NEW PRESSURES, NEW RESPONSES
IN RELIGIOUS LIFE

by

John P. Dondero, FSC, Ph. D.

&

Thomas D. Frary, Ph. D.

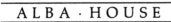

ALBA · HOUSE   NEW · YORK

SOCIETY OF ST. PAUL, 2187 VICTORY BLVD., STATEN ISLAND, NEW YORK 10314

Library of Congress Cataloging in Publication Data

Dondero, John P.
  New Pressures, New Responses in Religious Life.

  1. Monastic and religious life. I. Frary,
Thomas D., joint author. II. Title.
BX2435.D65   248'.894   76-26585
ISBN: 0-8189-0332-5

With Ecclesiastical Permission

Designed, printed and bound in the United States of
America by the Fathers and Brothers of the
Society of St. Paul, 2187 Victory Boulevard,
Staten Island, New York, 10314, as part of their
communications apostolate.

---

2 3 4 5 6 7 8 9 (Current Printing: first digit).

PREFACE

The title of this book, *New Pressures, New Responses in Religious Life*, hardly describes the depth and importance of its contents. The two authors have presented here their mutual reflections on the nature of religious life such as one seeks to live it today. Their joint effort is both complementary and intriguing. One of them is a religious, a specialist in physics, mathematics and psychology; the other is a lay theologian. Their "symbiotic" approach to the discussion makes their insights all the more significant.

This work will be of interest to all those preoccupied with the present-day evolution of religious life. The book has no intention of outlining rules of conduct or commands to be followed. Rather it is an analytical study focussed on the human behavior which undergirds religious life. It touches all the areas of concern in religious life today: the meaning of the vows, vocation, consecration, small communities, and many other topics as well.

This book also offers a much needed optimism in the face of today's failures and disappointments. The authors have a constructive approach to problems; for this reason alone the book deserves a wide audience.

We believe the future of religious communities will depend for the most part on the measure in which the Holy Spirit will be able to transform into a real "communion of life" what is only a juxtaposition or coexistence of individuals.

Loneliness, even at the very heart of religious community, seems to me to be the major problem of the future. The vitality of our communities will depend on the way in which that loneliness is conquered by the force and power of the Spirit. In the Canon of the Mass we ask that "the Spirit of the Lord make us one body." This is more important than ever before in today's communities. Psychology can and should help break down barriers to the realization of this communion. The spiritual life lived together at a deeper level and in reciprocal openness to one another will lead to that common spirit over and above all diversity among individuals.

The "vocation crisis" will have passed when young people have rediscovered Jesus as the greatest inspiration in their lives, as the Good News par excellence to be told to the world, and when they allow themselves to be radically transformed by His Spirit.

Malines, September 30, 1976

(Signed) L. J. Cardinal Suenens
Archbishop of Malines-Bruxelles

CONTENTS

INTRODUCTION

In the course of many visits to monasteries, houses of study and convents, and in innumerable discussions with members of the clergy and religious communities, one of the authors has been asked a persistent question: "As a psychologist, what do you predict for the future of religious life?" The temptation to play prophet is strong in such a circumstance for the concern which underlies the asking of the question assures an attentive ear to any pronouncement concerning this way of life. One could find the prophetic response quoted in many quarters as the current uncertainties about the religious life inch or gallop their way towards crisis proportions. In the reality of their life situation, present-day religious are genuinely concerned over the future of their way of life.

This real concern naturally evokes many official and unofficial pronouncements giving the *raison d'etre* of religious life. In the main, these are theological clarifications of the rationale underlying this way of life. They draw their explanations and justifications mainly from the New Testament, from history, and from the official documents of the Church. Occasionally, Old Testament writings and the written legacy of significant individuals long recognized for holiness will be added to buttress the force of the persuasive stance. There is no doubt that these treatises are needed and that they serve a useful purpose. However, modern scriptural exegesis suggests alternate meanings to many a quotation excerpted from scripture. Such different interpretations have the effect of introducing uncertainty into the effort to explain the basis of religious life. At least it would appear that these treatises do not seem to have saved the day. The lights have gone out in a number of religious communities and rectories. Men and women are responding to other calls to Christian living after once accepting membership in priesthood and/or religious life. The reduced ranks do not necessarily constitute a contravening argument to these treatises and pronouncements. We do not judge the value of this way of life merely in terms of the number of people currently "buying" it. Yet it may be possible to market a great product but if fewer and fewer people buy it, the appeal aspect of this "good" product has suffered a sharp decline.

The integrity of these official documents delineate religious life as it ought to be or as it might one day become—as conceptualized by the individual writers. The treatises are not written with the intention of describing religious life as it is—as it is experienced in the day-to-day existence of those who comprise its ranks. It would be difficult to live this form of life without some clear vision of what it might be, in the absence of some goal towards which it is hopefully moving. Whatever optimism or hope is generated by this vision of what might some day be seems to be unequal to the task of imparting present meaning to the lives of scores of men and women who opt for a different way of working out their Christian commitment after varying numbers of years in religious life.

These uncertainties in the Church affect all the People of God. The egress of priests and religious from their traditoinal way of life causes great consternation among some, causes others to be encouraged with a new hope that real issues are being confronted, and finds yet others with a couldn't-care-less attitude about what is happening. The publicity attendant to a change of life-style by a priest or religious is no longer a news scoop but still stays printworthy on the pages of newspapers. It is understandable why the laity wonder what is happening in the world of religion when dedicated people are opting out of form of life wherein conviction about spiritual values is the essence of that way of life. The laity are puzzled because they know that they have little or no chance to leave one status of life for another with anything near the ease with which priests and religious make the move. It seems that the Church more readily releases from Orders than from Matrimony. And for many religious, the tie to their way of life does not have the binding force of sacramental acceptance. Often, the cleanness of the separation in the realm of the religious life is not matched in the married life. So the laity wonder why it is that uncertainty decimates the best trained shock troops of the

Church.

Part of the difficulty stems from what is an effective dichotomy—at least at the level of formal perspective—between this life in the real world and what is called the spiritual life. Those in religious life are numerically small in comparison to the multitudes in what has come to be called the lay life. These lay people see religious life as being primarily concerned with the "world to come," as endeavoring to maintain contact and concern with the bread-and-butter issues of this world. Indeed when a religious ventures into the arena of social causes, the concern of laity and of Church demonstrates a mixed reaction—more often negative than positive. The dichotomy, again only at the level of perspective, seems to be a split in the existential concerns of religious life and of lay life. Alternately considering the two-life styles would lead to the admission that it is a matter of opinion as to whether here is an over-emphasis or an under-emphasis on the existential features of life. It is our view that focussing on the "here and now" or on the "there and then" to the exclusion of an intelligent acceptance of the alternative is likely to distort the reality of life on earth. This conviction will inform and underlie what is to be written in this book.

The "there and then" focus—that is, the living for a future— is important in that it can supply motivation for behavior in the "here and now." But one cannot live in the "there and then." The supernatural life is not something to be begun at some future date—perhaps at one's death. The sacramental waters of baptism have already initiated that life; it is "here and now." With St. Paul we may be seeing only dimly through a glass in a dark manner. Christ's invitation to the rich young man was a request (and a hope) that the life of the spirit could be lived in the "here and now"—informed by the "there and then."

As long as we continue to function under the difference of emphasis between the "there and then" and the "here and now" we will not move towards a resolution of the vocational crisis in our country. Both foci are essential and it is pointless to argue which of two essentials is the more important. For the human being, it is like asking which leg is the more important for walking.

Through the past year the two authors spent many hours in informal discussion of the many aspects of the issues facing the Church, religious life, and individuals in today's world. The ideas of this book are the outgrowth of their personal reflections about religious life. The views expressed find their roots in the existential or experiential realities of that life. In the work we have done during several years in separate parts of the country (one on the east coast and the other on the west coast) and especially in the work we did as members of a team working with a religious congregation four years ago, many specific problems facing religious life were confronted. Each of us has reflected on these problems in terms of our respective training and experience. The senior author (a religious) was awarded degrees in physics, in mathematics and in psychology and is a practicing psychologist with the doctorate degree. The junior author (a layman) was awarded the doctorate in theology and for many years was engaged in collegiate teaching; he has now entered the world of business wherein he is following his inclination to be a "market place theologian" in attempting to extend the application of theological knowledge to the realm of work, economics, married life.

Together we have discussed possible ways of looking at the important issues and problems facing religious life. Many of these discussions were entered into for our own understanding with no intent of turning to writing for the sake of sharing with others. Our discussions resulted from the attempts to clarify what our experience actually was and from the effort to understand what we were experiencing. From the vantage point of our respective disciplines we tried to make contributions to a common experience. On occasion the effort led to an understanding of the value and the functional aspect of religious life; on other occasions we came to understand the lack of value and the dysfunctional aspect of that life.

Now we want to share what we have thought in the hope that our views may provide some common understanding for those in religious life and for the laity in thinking about life. Perhaps such an understanding will contribute a measure of stability and vitality to that life for it is our belief that the vitality and stability of religious life depend importantly on both those within and those outside that life-style.

We do not plan a documented treatise since they already abound in sufficient number. Rather this joint work of a theologian and of a psychologist needs to "call it as it is" if the work is not to be somewhat abstract, assent-giving treatise that is soon filed and forgotten immediately after reading. Both disciplines run the risk of having their feet planted firmly in mid-air through over-theologizing and over-psychologizing. We hope to avoid this by focusing on the lived experience of religious life. Our work is not earmarked by the traditional erudition of the theologian doing an in-depth analysis of issues in Christian life nor by the technical jargon of the psychologist writing articles for professional journals. We hope to present two perspectives on problems of import. Possibly we might answer some questions; hopefully we will raise others. We have avoided stressing the speculative and yet have not presented a casebook of life histories to support our positions. We do not intend to suggest how things ought to be done in religious life.

Rather, one of our objectives is to alleviate confusion between what is theological and what is not, between what is psychological and what is not in the living out of religious life. We want to help those inside religious life take a fresh look; we want to help those outside to understand what is happening and how religious life fits into the total schema of the faith community. We share the view that the laity can say productive things about religious life since its roots are in their homes. Since one of the authors is a religious and the other is a layman, each brings a different perspective to the book. The layman is the theologian; the religious is the psychologist.

In yet another way our perspectives are different. One of us has exprienced religious life from within and has had many opportunities to closely work with and observe religious in other congregations from without. The layman on our team, having worked on the faculty of a small college run by a religious congregation, has been a very proximate viewer, meeting the consequences of the very existence of religious life and being directly influenced by its day-to-day functioning.

As a team, the authors are aware to a considerable extent that this book could easily become a medium for the expression of bias; we have also tried to state quite clearly when such bias colors our writing. This is a book which presents our points of view, our personal convictions, our attitudes. We desire to discuss basic issues rather than prescribe what-to-do directions on how to change religious life so as to be relevant to our times, so as to solve problems. We envision no canonized permanence to our views. Indeed, there was refinement, development and change as we worked together. We seek to explore ways of looking at issues in religious life which, we are convinced, need exploration or renewed emphasis.

We decided against each being responsible for alternate chapters in the book. If we could not discuss important issues in a way that would be readily intelligible to each other, we would have failed in a prime objective—that of writing for religious and laity in terms both can understand. To this end we have somewhat downplayed the speculative and theoretical approaches to religious life except for some brief sorties in writing about the nature of that life. Our preference and determination was to take our cues from our experience in working with religious and laity across the country. That experience includes close contact with religious communities in forty-three of the fifty states in the United States. Our point of departure is not the valuable theoretical formulations of theologians and psychologists; we rather believe we had better start with the lived experience of our American religious and laity.

We are led to the conclusion that there is indeed reason

to be optimistic about the future of religious life. We grant that our optimism is dependent on certain changes in beliefs and attitudes by both laity and religious. But because these changes, if they occur, will bring a greater union with each other and hence with God, we count on the efficacy of new understanding to give a resurgence to religious life, perhaps in numbers, but surely in meaning and vitality for all the People of God.

NEW PRESSURES, NEW RESPONSES
IN RELIGIOUS LIFE

1

Perspectives on Vocation

IN A COUNCIL SPEECH to the hierarchy for Vatican II, Bishop Gerard Hugghe spoke in part about a number of confusions in dealing with the evangelical counsels. One such misrepresentation would be to think that the "counsels are not proposed for all Christians but only for a select few, for religious." Vatican II clearly repudiates such an affirmation. Christ proposes the evangelical counsels to all his disciples—not to just a few. In view of this universal call, the men and women in religious life cannot be said to be doing something to which they alone have been called in living out, as best they can, the evangelical counsels. They are rather trying to respond to Christ's universal invitation to move with growing freedom to the perfection of love. The universality of the invitation by Christ is in no way circumscribed by the current debate over just which of the counsels have scriptural support.

Perhaps the uniqueness so often attributed to religious life is to be established in the means taken to live out the counsels. Here we speak of the vows. These are the acts of free men and women who freely and in a public manner desire and so attest to dedicate themselves to the pursuit of Christ's universal invitation. Because the vows are a means, the persons who take on themselves their obligations are therefore constituted professional religious. They have given public testimony of their commitment to live the counsels in the precise way spelled out by their particular congregation and by the Church in and of a particular historical period. There is, however, a danger in conceptualizing religious life in this way. It is the danger, as Bishop Hugghe points out, of identifying the evangelical counsels with the vows of religious life. They are not the same at all. The counsels clearly precede the vows. The vows permit the religious to formalize their commitment to live out the counsels.

They obligate the religious to certain behaviors which, in the main, would be the logical consequence of an earnest living out of the counsels. The vows concretize and specify the effort to live the counsels.

What does a person do when pronouncing vows? The person believes first that he/she has been called by God, called to consecrate his/her whole life to the single-minded task of professing, either publicly or privately, the evangelical counsels He/she believes that this consecration, motivated by love of God, is not so much something other than his/her baptismal consecration but is a further call from God to intensify this baptismal consecration and maximize that grace. He/she believes that the special character of the call and of religious life rests in the fact that the evangelical counsels, infused with charity, are the ultimate witness to the presence in this world of the kingdom that is God's. He/she believes that in the actual professing of the evangelical counsels he/she is indeed more intimately bound both to God and to the Church—to God because of the grace of this call—to the Church because its singular purpose is to witness to the advent and the building of the kingdom of God. Accordingly, the person believes and senses that he/she has placed self in a new and different relationship with the human social organization. The person, by taking vows, personally places self under new obligations in a relationship that is now different, requiring, obviously, a grace special to the type of commitment being made.

We are persuaded that much of the debate about vows stems from a very incomplete and untenable view of the psychological nature of the commitment. Assuming the theological basis of commitment (a topic to be discussed later) we would like to focus on the realities of commitment from the psychological viewpoint. It is important to allow this narrowing of perspective for there is a rigidity of focus that necessarily follows upon the acceptance of vows as having the nature of contract with the social organization. While there are some ambiguities even there, we want to avoid discussing the binding contractual nature of vows taken with a social organization and in compliance to the rules and regulations of that organization. The problem is not so much the theological underpinnings of vowing, but rather the grace-filled, though still human, condition in which they are practiced.

A clarification is needed at the outset. The taking of vows in religious life is an act that addresses the behavioral side of social living. Vowing is behavior-oriented. However much one may argue that vowing would seem meaningless unless informed by values accepted as underpinnings to the promise to behave in prescribed ways, it is still the undeniable truth that it is behavior which is promised in vow, a behavior patterned on the charity of Jesus Christ, but nonetheless still behavior. It is also true that patterned behavior makes personal sense only if its motivation is consonant with the behavior engaged. The love of God and of neighbor conjointly inform the behavior promised in vow. It has always seemed amusing to note how, in general, those in religious life are usually appalled at the tenets of behaviorism as a psychological theory when applied in life, in the classroom, in therapy—and yet are willingly involved in an encompassing life-style in which behavior regulation and control are at its very foundation. Once a person promises to behave in prescribed ways, it is the next easy and logical step for authorities to claim to have the right to structure the life situations so that only the vowed behavior is likely to be manifest. Long before the term became popular, religious life was adept at "behavior modification." Often enough the modification was so thorough that people became unable to function effectively as responsible persons when tasks of leadership and decision were given to them.

But behavior does not take place in a vacuum. Its context is the entire fabric of life at the given historical moment at which the behavior is to be enacted. As an illustration, the changing picture of Catholic education here in America will have vast effects on the behavior of religious—effects which the individual religious cannot control. Women's liberation, while perhaps not directly influencing the question of celibacy, will have consequences in the area of human relationships and behavior of those in religious life. If behavior is pressured toward modification as the result of forces operative within the context in which that behavior is to take place, it is logical to argue that future change, whether fierce or mild, can be expected to alter behavior in some manner. It would seem that any specific behaviors vowed in 1977 might be inappropriate in 1999—all the while leaving untouched the motivating dynamic of love of God and neighbor. The escape from this suggestion of instability is the recourse to the "principles" underlying the vow.

We hope that it is clear that we hold that the theological motivation for taking vows is love of God. It is true that this personal love can be both motivation to live a certain way as well as the source of modifications for that very living—fasting, praying, meditating, reading, volunteering, etc. Vows, when taken in a religious congregation, are an institutional modification of a person's desire to love God. And within that institutional framework, how the vows are applied or interpreted can either foster the individual's search for love of God or hinder it.

At the heart of the vows is the matter of commitment. This commitment is to the love of God. However, if one can also see a function of the vows as regulating behavior, then commitment becomes more readily understood and less problematic. For a person is either behaving according to promise or is not so behaving. The psychological components of commitment are inconsequential in this behavioral address to the vows. This is more than just a bit unpalatable in the task of living life; it seems much too narrow. Casuists, seeking to rescue the vowed life from this restrictive viewpoint, sometimes insert the idea of degree of behavior conformity and, hence, allow for talking about degree of commitment. Rather it is with the concept and reality of motivation (not the reality of behavior) that the meaning of commitment has the most trouble. No one can insure that one's current motivation will be functional at some specific future moment in one's personal history. In a legalistic and in a theological sense one can bind self to behaviors in the future. From a psychological standpoint the actual meaning of such a "binding" is difficult to pinpoint. No one can say with certitude that "I am going to be as convinced in 1999 of this particular value as I am now in 1977." Regardless of whether a person "takes" temporary or perpetual vows, he/she is saying "I endorse *now* this particular value, I promise this particular behavior; I inform my life by this value *now*; it seems so good to me now that I hope that value shall always so regulate and inform my life." Commitment is a *now* phenomenon for the psychologist. From that viewpoint, one can make a commitment now about the future but one cannot now make a commitment in the future. Psychology aside, the Church, if only because it is God's grace that is involved, acknowledges that individuals can make life-long commitments.

Try, if you can, to spell out the difference in commitment between the person who takes temporary vows and the person who takes perpetual vows. Certainly, in daily living, there are no differences that can be delineated. The vowed behavior is identical in each case and, hopefully, the values informing the vows are quite similar. But perhaps temporary vows tend to imply a lesser, degree of commitment. Psychologically, that is a rather incomprehensible statement. If they do, then the failure to "keep" the vows must also be of lesser consequence. Religious life does not accept such casuistry. The tie between the temporality-perpetuality continuum and the degree of commitment is a dangerous one because it says nothing about commitment itself but tries to operationally define it in time-span terms. Would the commitment implied in a "for one week" vow be any different than the commitment implied in a "for one year" vow—in a "for three years" vow? If so, what are the differences? If a person dies while in temporary vows, has his/her commitment been any different from the one dying with perpetual vows? If so, how? The posing of this series of questions suggests the position of the authors—there really are no substantive differences.

It could be argued that religious life rather subconsciously knows there are no differences in those commitments per se. So, this life added prerogatives and privileges successively to each step in the ladder of vow taking—right to vote, right to hold office, etc. This implied that there are indeed differences in commitment to be associated with vows taken for longer periods of time. On the other hand, if having vows for longer spans of time is somehow to be associated with maturity of judgment, then the fairness of binding by vow for whatever short time period is debatable since the obligations when so bound tolerate no reduction in scope or force.

Religious life has witnessed hundreds of its members joyfully and honestly bind themselves by vow *forever*. Yet from the ranks of these same people, scores upon scores seek dispensation from their vows. What, really, does it mean to say they were vowed perpetually when, in fact, they no longer are? Perpetual vows have meaning when they work—by that we mean, that if a person dies when so vowed, then the vows are indeed perpetual. But surely they are not perpetual in anticipation. Commitment is a *now* phenomenon and a *now* experience. Commitment with a future orientation is really not an active decision presently functional in the future (an impossibility in any frame) but is rather a hope, a dream, a desire.

Since Christ's invitation was to all persons, it can be said that the living of the counsels does not require the taking of vows. While vowed commitment to live the counsels may be the distinguishing characteristic of religious life, one must be cautious about allowing the taking of vows to be the primary significant action of that life. Rather it is the living of the counsels which is primary. According to Christ, this could be done without the vows. The making of vows in support of one's desire to live the counsels places the person under new obligations. The vows are in the nature of an obligation in one's relationship to God. The religious responded to a call to be "different" by doing the counsels differently—namely, by vowing them in the Church. The religious enters a unilateral contract with God and therefore stands in a new relationship with God. But God is not under any new obligation towards the religious except in fulfillment of His promise to offer the special graces to live that life.

In the Dogmatic Constitution on the Church, the Church says that a person in religious life has a "special title" and that religious are joined "to the Church and her mystery in a special way." But in no sense does the Church call religious a special people, neither in the sense of some new state between clergy and laity, nor in the sense that others in the Church are just plain and ordinary. The word "special" is not to be used to set one Christian off against the other; it is not to be used in a qualitative sense referring to a particular individual contrasted to another as higher or better. The Church in even its highest authority cannot make that judgment. Nor does the Church say that religious are joined to God in a special relationship. A special (read, particularized) grace of God is indeed necessary and granted to one embracing the vowed life in religion. But who in the Church does not receive special graces? In the context in which the Church uses the word, the specificity is not in some kind of newly created relationship with God, but rather in the intensifying of an already existing relationship. The specialness toward God is in the intimacy established by living with total abandonment the life and example of His Son, Jesus. But such specialness of intimacy is open to all God's people and all are called to it. We believe that in the teaching of the Church, the word "special" has not only the above theological content but also reflects the mother's pride in a child who has been chosen by God to do something different. In this sense "special" addresses itself to a relationship set up between the individual and the Church. That relationship is indeed special in that it provides stability and proven ways in the achievement of intimacy with God.

Religious, in referring in any public forum to their way of life, more often than not will use such a word as "consecrated" to differentiate their life style from that of others. Because of this they readily accept the status of "special people" accorded them by the laity. They are even protected by canonical laws which entrench the idea of being special. The existence of this attitude and belief on the part of the laity is a matter of historical record. And the acceptance of this belief and attitude by the religious is also a matter of record. Such a condition becomes understandable when one accepts the truth and the reality experience that it is a dreadful thing to wrestle with a jealous God for one's very life; it is a dreadful thing to have to assent to the cost of the love of God, to the evangelical demand of self-renunciation. So, when the laity, against this background of their own experience, see a group of men or women publicly affirm a determination to contend with this God, they accord them an esteem and veneration that is supportive to their own efforts to relate to God. It is also self-protective in that it becomes a belief (often promoted by the religious) that not all men and women are invited by Christ to such radical self-renunciation. That is obviously a false conclusion. Holding God at arm's length by "letting the religious be the ones who totally respond to the invitation" becomes subjectively justified for the laity if the religious themselves hold this unique view of their own vocation.

In this connection, the use of the term "consecrated" in speaking of the religious life may lead to a misinterpretation of the nature of the commitment to Christ. Yet the Church uses the term "special consecration" in the Decree on Religious Life but its meaning seems to be an act by the individual in taking the vows. It is not a consecration from without, not a consecration by another or by the Church. There are no formal acts of consecration exercised by the Church in accepting the written vow statements as acknowledgement that the religious have been bound to certain behaviors in their desire to live the counsels. It is not a consecration of the same kind as in baptism, confirmation, holy orders, episcopacy.

Still the Church declares that religious are consecrated

persons. But it is only in a restricted or special sense that this status of "consecrated" is extended to religious. In Paragraph 5 of the Decree on Religious Life of Vatican II, the Church speaks of religious in these terms:

> They have handed over their entire lives in an act of special consecration which is deeply rooted in their baptismal consecration and which provides an ample manifestation of it.

As a consequence of his/her baptismal consecration, an individual in response to God's call can opt to accept a radicalization of both his/her baptismal consecration and his/her commitment to God. To do this publicly, to do this within and before the Church is an act of consecration. Certainly this is different within the Church in the sense that the frequency of such consecrations is small when compared to the total membership. Nor does this say that this radical response is not found among others than religious. The further differentiation is that the one consecrated submits self to the Church and its proven ways of sustaining such a consecration.

It is part of revelation and Christian tradition that vocation as used in the Christian community has its primary meaning in that activity in which God takes the initiative and, subsequently, in mankind's response to that initial activity. All other theological meaning is drawn from this primary meaning. In this sense, vocation is indeed a call, for God is the initiator and the call does carry an imperative with eternal consequences for the person. The call is to stand in a relationship to the Holy—not distanced and alienated but in the intimacy and trust of a child. The call is to become His son, His daughter.

This definitive call is further specified for the Christian in terms of baptism. But with baptism some difficulties to understanding the call may arise. The invitation and response to the initial call is more in the nature of a confrontation between person and God in a one-to-one relationship with no intervening authority, no intervening community to be responsible to, no history of the need for the community to render differing services, no history of how that initial vocation can or will be lived out, no comfort in a life shared. The call and its anticipated response finds the person standing alone. To be in this one-to-one relationship is a precarious and ambiguous position in that the person has no guidelines for living his sonship, her daughtership, no directives for being son or daughter. It is profoundly awesome to be invited to such a relationship with the Holy. Because of His love for us, God has initiated and established channels through which His love call alleviates the precariousness of this magnificent yet overwhelming invitation.

Born into a world of other human beings, the Christian finds that the stark reality of the invitation to sonship or daughtership is tempered by all the social realities of human existence. There is authority; there is community; there are guidelines; there is the comfort of shared life of a people. When the Christian responds in baptism to that initial call to be God's son or daughter, he or she enters into the relationship of a community which is going to demand of the person and will specify for the person the further dimensions of the response to the initial call.

The call to be God's son or daughter is first of all specified sacramentally. Through this means the relationship to the Father is more deeply and personally clarified—as son or daughter in baptism, as filled with the Holy Spirit in confirmation, as repentant and forgiver in penance, as sharing the gift of God's life and the mystery of redemption extended to all persons in the Eucharist, etc. It is this sacramental life that remains the abiding element of vocation within the Christian community no matter by what name the various communities are identified. Beyond the sacramental life, all differences between groups are accidental differences. Additional determinations of this sacramental response are left to the charismatic judgment of the Church and to the individual Christian, alone or in cooperation with a group.

Vocation in the Church is not a thing. It is not a thing

someone can lose, or find, or break, or water. Vocation is an event, it is a happening. It is the dynamic response between a caller and a called. Vocation in the Church remains and shall remain both mystery and reality—mystery because it is The Holy who calls; reality because the Church guided by the Holy Spirit acknowledges *persons* responding to God's call. The folly of trying to reify vocation is clear if one is asked to point out a vocation. It was not unheard of in the history of religious life that obedience to commands was often achieved under the implication that any contrary behavior would invite the risk of "losing one's vocation" and, by further extension, in "incurring the displeasure of God." The one displeasure actually experienced was that of the command giver; what action God took remained an indeterminable reality. An implication was that God will take away what he once gave and with enduring adverse consequences.

The basic problem in recognizing God's call is its mystery, its lack of common sense clarity. One of the reasons why there is such uncertainty in this matter lies in the subtle but effective segmentation that goes on when one tries to acquire vision of his/her relationship with God.

One of the great gifts conferred on human beings by God is the gift of freedom. Yet in matters not sinful, we seem to be short-changing the same God by implying that He would not at all be satisfied with the selection of either alternative in a free choice situation. If not that, then we seem to imply a rather deterministic operation on God's part if we conceptualize vocation as a thing allowing only one course of action or response by that person. Our human tendency to impose our human categories of judgment, evaluation, and behavior on our God has to be watched very carefully if we would come to understand religious vocation. The fuzziness of our thinking can be thickened by introducing the reality of the grace of God into our attempt to understand. We ought not praise God for the freedom that He gave us and then adopt a deterministic, choose-rightly-or-else stance in regard to religious vocation.

In its charismatic function the Church can and must present criteria to assure itself (as well as the responder to God's call) that such a call is present. It is the Church and not the individual alone that makes this authentication. Furthermore these criteria must originate from the historical life of the Church and therefore be open not simply to past historical experience but also to present experience of the Holy Spirit in the Church. At the psychological level, one's movement towards entrance into a particular congregation has no unique features which would differentiate it from movement towards any other work or state in life. Whatever unique characteristics there might be fail to make themselves obvious anywhere along the route. To imply the existence of a thing called vocation, to fail to announce definitive signs of its existence prior to entering religious life, to impute unworthy or base motivation for failure to cooperate with this "thing," to set a no-alternative limitation to response, to make decisions by others the criterion of its true existence—all these stances introduce such confusion that a considerable challenge to psychological health is meted out to the person caught in the barrage of these would-be truths. The uncertainties are kept under control as long as the segmentation of concepts, realities, and errors can be maintained. It is precisely because this segmentation is not very effective or long lasting that a reaction against this fragmented living frequently comes about.

We have come to believe that the marked concerns in the past decade about "fulfillment" achieved a ready response within the ranks of religious men and women not because religious life had proved incapable of facilitating this fulfillment but rather as a reaction to this segmented intellectualization on the nature of vocation and on the response of men and women to the realities of this way of life. A good example of the convenience of this compartmentalization of ideas about vocation is found in the stout claim that it is God who calls, irrevocably, on a one-to-one basis, on a never-to-be-refused premise of acceptance by the person called. Yet it is incumbent on the religious themselves to pass judgment, in admitting a person to vows, on whether or not another human being is indeed called by God. For many religious there doesn't appear to be any contradiction here. Apparently only by dying in the saddle will one offer proof that he/she had a true vocation in the first place. If unseated by the action of others, he/she never had a vocation in the first place. By easy extension of this idea, if a person, having once entered religious life, then opts by personal choice for another life style, "he/she never had a vocation" or, worse, "he/she did not pray enough or lead a spiritual enough life." Enough seems to mean whatever is sufficient to maintain membership.

In the present and recent past in religious life the word "defection" is used to identify the action of persons leaving religious life. That usage is inappropriate. Why cannot God call an individual to religious life at one period in that person's sacred history and out of His love for that individual call him/her to something other at another period? Why cannot God utilize religious life experience, even for years, and have it become a leaven called elsewhere in His kingdom. After all, the Church certainly is not exactly the kingdom, yet it is the kingdom that God wishes and the Church serves. Why cannot God be involved in what is presently happening?

The emphasis on vocation as so clearly supernatural, as so munificently beyond the human choice of man, as the irrefutable indication of God's predilection for particular individuals over other individuals could only result in awe responses by humans. It at once removed the necessity for integration of the concepts we have been discussing along with the lived experience of those in religious life which must also be integrated into our understanding. It is our conviction that the rethinking of all aspects of religious vocation, a process to be informed by current theological and psychological thought, will result in a clear optimism about the future of religious life. As the authors, both the theologian and the psychologist have reached this conclusion. We intend to show the thoughts which led us to this optimism.

It is also our persuasion that this rethinking cannot be the exclusive concern of those already within or those considering entrance into religious life. The future of religious life is intimately dependent upon the understandings of the laity and upon the inescapable fact that they are already involved in terms of their interaction with the one People of God whose lives crisscross their own. Therefore this book is directed as much to the laity as it is to those in religious life.

Thus we can speak of membership in a community and have our words be applicable to all men and women. The man or woman who lives alone (if one such could be found) is to a great extent dependent only on self; he/she bends only in terms of self, in terms of personal needs. The risks taken are risks that he/she alone has gauged, that he/she alone has decided to take with the knowledge that they must be faced alone.

But when a man or woman joins a community, he/she accepts more than personal dependence. The acceptance is of a dependency on the community, on people who might be unknown personally. He/she becomes involved in needs that are not one's own. Membership in community makes the needs of that community part of his/her own needs. The risks of the larger group are accepted, sometimes never knowing the extent of all those risks. But more importantly he/she has so involved the personal response to that initial call to become a son/daughter of God in the total response of a community that he/she no longer is an individual responding without any bonds but rather is a member of a Christian community, a people, answering that call.

Within the Christian community, that call is specified by baptism. It is the sacramental action of the community—its initiation ceremony. Baptism does not antedate the call to sonship, to daughtership. But the baptismal commitment to this Christian community and to the Lord who has fathered it is determinative of any further response to that initial call. For certain, God's call remains in that community, initially to become His son/daughter, but is now specified in many ways as to how that response can be made within this community while keeping true to the initial call. The Christian will also respond to the needs of the community itself and to the needs of the world in which it finds itself at any given moment. After baptism God's call manifests itself through the community and through the world in which that community lives, exercises its life potential and tries to respond to the initial call.

If the Christian individual were to attempt to heed God's call apart from the complexity, history, needs, hopes and desires of his/her community in this world, he/she would need to follow the single mandate, "Be my son/daughter." That might be of some solace and encouragement to the individual were it not for the fact that its premise is a false "if" statement. God's call is not made under the premised conditions. God does not enter this world from some vantage point up in the sky. He is a God of history, entering mankind's life not merely in terms of starting the whole process in the acts of creation. He is not a booming voice occasionally startling humans in periodic entrance from a distant kingdom. He speaks to mankind only in the real history of people in this one world. If the individual listens within this community at the particular moment in the world in which the people live, he/she sees open a variety of ways of responding to that call. Thus it is that priesthood and the married life become in that community sacramental specifications of that call. They are necessary to the essential life of the Church—the one of sacramental service and service of the word to the community; the other to witness to the mystery of the relation between Christ and the Church. But there are also other responses. One such additional response is the religious life which has been sanctioned by the Church. Still another response, the single life, seems to have been forgotten for some reason. At most, little is ever said about it.

There has been a history in the Church of according a hierarchy of holiness to the priesthood, to religious life and to the lay (married) life in descending order. This no longer stands for it is now clearly recognized that the call to holiness in the Church is to all alike and that no particular position in the organizational structure (often viewed as some holiness hierarchy) of the Church is any assurance as to sanctity. We have come to the time when the status of ascription (the affirmation of personal worth and/or holiness as equated with position) is no longer the mode of viewing individuals among the People of God. The initial call is the same for all who accept the initial vocation given in baptism. It is specified for the married couple and for the priest and sets for each of them the distinctive manner in which they respond to that vocation.

But what of single persons. The Church's answer for them was the religious life, not as an alternative to being single but simply because some people did not choose either the married life or the priesthood but who still wished to have their life be a specific witness. It is important to note that it was not the Church that created this kind of life out of a need for some people to find a way of specifying their Christian life with as clear a witness dimension as found in marriage or the priesthood. The religious life is one answer to the quest for a channel of acceptance of God's invitation. Perhaps the nature of vocation will come into even clearer perspective through considering that oft forgotten state of the single person.

The thesis here is that vocation is indeed a grace-filled call to differing forms of service and witness in the Church. It is a call not clearly heard because of necessity it must involve mystery, God's mystery. It is a call that includes the charismatic judgment of the Church. It is a call to the individual to find, within the expanse of this community which he/she became part of through baptism, where he/she might best fullfill the initial call, given to baptism, prior to Church, and now specified in baptism to be God's son/daughter. This seems to be the task of all Christians—to try for a more ample manifestation of the grace of baptism. Religious vocation is the call to the person to complete this manifestation by joining himself/herself intimately to the Church's mission through vowing the evangelical counsels.

The special nature of religious life is vainly sought if the source is thought to be holiness—all members of the Christian community are called to the same holiness. It is vainly sought if it is expected to be found in an obvious position of authority. It is vainly sought if it is considered a position of privilege rather than a position of service. The specialness of religious life is not simply in God's call to intimacy with Himself for He can call anyone to that and often does so. The specialness of religious life is the response to a call to seek that intimacy precisely in the evangelical counsels and to do so publicly, in rather stable circumstances and by ways found valid and fruitful in the Church

If one is seeking intimacy with God he/she is responding to God's call to all His people. Some ways are more cluttered, less sure in direction, more circuitous in route, more open to interference, subject to the vagaries of a kingdom yet to come. What the Church offers in recognizing religious life as a call to this intimacy is its lack of clutter (hopefully), its directionalness (hopefully), its straight and narrow approach (again, hopefully). But this is to be achieved only at a tremendous cost—the cost of one's whole life.

Vocation itself, in a sense, doesn't exist. A God who calls does. Persons who respond do. Vocation in the Church's life was recognized only as the call and response were lived out, worked at and completed. The Church learned of it primarily in its being done. Vocation is essentially two persons becoming involved in a call-response relationship—God and a human being. Vocation is an active situation—not just a state of life. And as an active situation it is open to change, possible of new responses. Vocation exists only when there is a God in His situation and a man/woman in his/her own situation. Ordinarily that is a very complicated situation.

The person who responds to the initial vocation by loving his/her neighbor is in the process of accepting that invitation. Or it can be put another way—that person who loves his/her neighbor is acting out the universal vocation whether that person knows it or not, whether that person knows God or not. If there is anything special about vocation after this, it is simply that I have looked at myself, at the world in which I live, at the Church of which I am part, at the call I believe I hear, and have decided that for me this particular way is better for my living out the commitment to the Church and the gospel that I accepted in baptism.

2
Revitalization of Religious Life

IN THE ACTIVE RELIGIOUS CONGREGATIONS, the life-style in community living is a compromise concerning those spiritual and service functions that are sufficiently respectable and marketable so as to warrant their institutionalization. Any change in that life-style is difficult because religious communities exist, in large measure, for the sake of order in human life. They function to routinize behavior and interaction between people. They succeed in this goal because those who compose the community generally believe in what they are doing. Perhaps in these days it is better to hold that they believe in the possibility that living in community may be a support to their effort to discern the working of the Spirit in their lives. If the hoped for support is not part of their experience, there is small expectation that they will remain within the particular community.

Social organizations tend to develop more commitment to their personnel and procedures than to their purpose. On the surface of things, the commitment to personnel seems to be the focus of concern by many religious today. There is indeed a need for more personalized concern and interaction for the lack of such concern has speeded the departure of many from their communities. Yet it is to be hoped that religious life would show a consistency in its concern for personnel. A concern which is only loosely tied to the purposes of the organization or a concern tied tightly or loosely to selected purposes is more constrictive than liberating. When growth and development in one's personal relationship with God are overlooked in favor of fostering community life, there has been an inversion which will eventually result in conflict. When one's attention to personnel is interpreted in terms of this unrealized inversion, the original means adopted to accomplish ends slowly become goals. That statement is in-

tended to suggest the mistake and the folly of making the a-
chievement of a sense of community a primary goal of the effort
to live a full spiritual life within a community. If such a goal is
endorsed, innovations that would increase personal growth can
easily be rejected. Much of the negative feeling about the movement towards smaller satellite communities has its roots in this
inversion. It is a paradox that much of the motivation of those
opting for these very same smaller communities is also found
in the desire for closer community relationships. So both the
opposition and the advocates draw their weapons from the same
source. This often occurs as a community, as a province, as a
congregation goes through the steps of authorizing changes by
means of vote-outcome by a legislative assembly. At that moment passive resistance is born which can become continuous,
pervasive and insidious. Any vote in religious community is often
preliminary to the real battle. But once taken, any reversal of
that vote is but one new challenge to resistance by yet another
group. Many religious, having moved into a satellite community
after having received approbation from all the required offices
and committees, find remnants of disdain and hostility to be part
of the attitude of large numbers of the community. Religious life
has not accommodated itself very well at all to the democratic
governance. We in no way argue that governance in religious
life should be democratic. We simply state that efforts at democratic organization have not fared very well. Religious life has
been favorable to decentralization of authority in its adulthood-
achieved reaction. But the battle only began there.

It is a widely accepted sociological dictum that change and
innovation tend to stem from individuals who are "marginal" to
current practices, to current stances. Marginality allows a greater
degree of rejection of the codes of behavior in one's surroundings. Those religious who are marginal people are the religious
who are willing to take risks and so firm thrusts for innovations
can be expected. It follows that the safe way to protect religious
life from the pressure to change is to isolate or repudiate the
marginal member. Subtle and often not so subtle campaigns of

implication that the marginal member is "bordering on unfaithfulness and disloyalty" or that the member is "already on the way out and is therefore repudiating us faithful ones" are not uncommon in religious communities across the country. Little growth or development can be expected from those communities who keep closing ranks against the marginal member. And this leaves aside the question of whether such closedness can be reconciled with Christianity.

One of the frustrations of these marginal members is that they are not given the opportunity to buttress their positions and ideas with the testimony of "experts" to the same extent as nonmarginal members have this chance. These "experts" who endorse the same views as the marginal members could perhaps better express the thoughts and ideas and do so with less antagonism from and repudiation by the traditionalist religious. But the in-power members control the purse strings and the invitational rights as to which "experts" eventually address, evaluate, or point the direction of government. And if such government thinks it operates without bias, without succumbing to selective procedures supportive of its preferred position, it has lost touch with its own reality. We can attest to such careful selection of speakers, retreat masters, and teachers within some congregations so that only one point of view is ever heard—that supporting the present government of the congregation. And yet it is strongly argued that there is participatory government. Democracy in religious life is more often than not a euphemism for a (hopefully) benevolent dictatorship. How quickly religious forget that their founders had such difficulty getting a hearing, that they, too, were considered rather marginal people in the scheme of things.

To preserve religious life unchanged in the face of a decline in membership one must either assure a captive audience for it— for example, by requiring total conformity by all members—or amass persuasive arguments of a spiritual nature that avoid the necessity of concern over a market for this way of life. Under pressure to conform, little creative or innovative thinking and behavior will be possible since deviations from normative standards are summarily dealt with. The "God-will-provide" stance is an assumption of the coercive role on the part of God in the free-choice response to vocation. More and more has the call to reestablish firm structures and behavioral rules been heard as reaction to the loosening process of the past several years.

To take refuge in the reassuring arms of either stance is to ignore the realities of what is actually happening. The numbers in seminaries and houses of formation are down; the depletion in the ranks of those already in active ministries is quite real. The captive audience seems to have a survival motif at its base. On the other hand, while the spiritual principles argument is true, it has a tendency to ignore the reality that unless there are people around who accept the principles we still do not have a viable religious life.

If there is to be any expectation of change from within religious life, the norms functioning for the congregation have to be studied. A congregation may have arrived at a point in its development where its standards are deemed to be the best possible standards for regulating behavior. Having the stamp of approval of the Church, these standards are judged to be unexcellable. Thus it comes about that any proposed change of standards seems, necessarily, to be a lowering of standards. Only the traditional is legitimate; the untraditional is illegitimate. As a congregation comes to be viewed as good or sacred in itself, any advocacy of change is rejected as evil. Change would be detrimental to historic obligation, to the essence of the congregation, to the founder-inspired spirit of the institutional purpose; the congregation has taken the first steps towards fossilization. Holding to tradition for the sake of holding is unwarranted. Traditions which have a current viability in their own right will survive without making their perdurance an institutional purpose. Traditions with current meaning have a staying power of their own; they do not need the concretizations of laws to remain viable, nor the fierce determination of self-styled guardians of tradition to remain instructive and informative. If seen in historical perspective, they invite their own continuance or their own adaptation to present circumstances.

One of the prime contributing factors to the current trouble in religious life is found in the conflictual situation which sets "spiritual" values against human values. Pursuant to their desire to dedicate themselves to God, the religious grant an immediate ascendency to motives which are "supernatural"—despite the puzzlement as to how a human, natural entity can have a supernatural human nature. One of the great needs for revitalizing religious life is the need for clarification of the language used in speaking about it. The word "'supernatural" is one such word requiring clarification. Much of what is written in this book contributes, it is our hope, to increased understanding. Any enterprise undertaken out of love of God and in service of His people under the mantle of religious life seems to imbed, quite automatically, the view that its supernatural intent will always overcompensate for any necessity for entering into enterprises with all the wisdom, acumen, and strategies of a specifically human enterprise.

The search for new forms of government in religious life may illustrate this point. It appears that religious life still lacks an effective form of government. Movements in favor of decentralization, of subsidiarity, of participatory democracy are in vogue nowadays. Yet to every one of these thrusts there arises a counter thrust for maintaining the status quo or for grudgingly conceding movement along one dimension while retracting along another. Thus we see decentralization in those matters not crucial to the maintenance of the organization as an organization but a move towards centralized control in matters considered essential to the organizational structure. Latitude is sought and granted in the area of the spiritual life of individuals and community but centralization of financial aspects is becoming more widely employed. When honesty faces the realization that religious life is far from utopian in its exercise of government an escape from this all-too-human condition is found in an appeal to the workings of the Holy Spirit. Calling upon the Spirit (salvation by rhetoric alone) seems to absolve all religious, particularly those governing, of their quite human, sinful, biased and prejudiced conditions. Thus there is no prejudice in any government that calls upon the Spirit to direct all its decisions and edicts. It is somewhat amusing to note the discomfort of many religious if a meeting is not opened with a prayer. One might wonder if serious reflection at the end of a meeting would convince all participants of the unequivocal evidence of the action of the Spirit in all that transpired during that meeting.

Once the close identification is made between the action of the Holy Spirit and the decisions of the one in the position of responsibility, challenges to the exercise of responsibility are almost automatically seen as challenges to the personal responsibility of that individual. If steadfastness is not maintained against the choice of a different course of action (for surely the former is what the Spirit wants), there will be consequent eternal repercussions for that individual. One result of this close identification between activity of the Spirit and the personal values and preferences of the governor is that the individual commitment of the leader has suddenly become the commitment of the entire community. But the point cannot be stressed too forcibly that it is the religious themselves who have asked for such a development with their essentially naive attitude toward government. Happily there are some indications that this is changing, but there is still a great distance to go.

Currently, religious life is thrusting towards a more democratic form of government. It is the limited scope of this thrust which will bring a whole new bag of problems, since what is being sought is only a portion of the democratic process. A bits-and-pieces form of democracy may spawn more problems than it solves while being a poultice to selected complaints about government. If a secular pattern of government is going to be assumed, it cannot be assumed effectively without those necessary sanctions that support civil government. There is no real delegation of authority, no real participation in government without consequent sanctions on that acceptance of participatory authority. Since the government we are here talking about is a practical functioning of human beings in the practical order, those sanctions must bear practical effect. Divine sanctions are not known to be the most coercive in producing secular or civil government. Along with the sharing of decision must go the sharing of responsibility for the consequences.

The stress on the responsibility of those in authority has to be balanced by a similar stress on the part of those governed. One of the more obvious blind-spots in the conduct of the affairs of the apostolate in religious life is that of personal responsibility. Men and women in religious life live and operate in a very protective environment. In recent years there has been a move in the direction of delegation of authority, but there does not seem to have been the concomitant allocation of responsibility. If a religious botches a job given to him/her, there is always a cushion to fall back on. There is always the parent organization which will pour balm into the wounds, cover over the botch, take upon itself the major blame for the outcome, cite the mysterious workings of the Holy Spirit, utter words of consolation.

The chronicle of religious life is filled with instances of individuals who were notoriously inept in positions in schools, hospitals, and other works of the apostolate. We have not as yet come to the point where a religious who does a poor job, who makes mistakes or who may totally botch a job assumes total responsibility for his/her performance. It is at such a point that the "spiritual" values spring to the forefront, prompting the congregation to take the protective stance that when a person enters religious life he/she has done something so wonderful, so unselfish that such dedication and consecration far outweigh all other areas of human enterprise. The religious is protected against the necessity of confronting personal failures. The situation is further compounded by the fact that even if the other members clearly see the ineptitude, they are restrained from pushing for change since anything done of a critical nature reflects (it is presumed) their own level of meager spirituality.

It is our thought that this state of affairs is the result of a misconception of the nature of religious vocation.

Another indication of this built-in security blanket is the great facility which exists among religious for blame-placing on persons somewhat removed from the scene of conflict. It is the lack of foresight at the next higher level of administration that accounts for the present unfortunate situation. Under normal circumstances, the religious rarely if ever goes to the immediate superior with the statement that "you really botched that job." Rather we hear "I wonder what ever possessed the Provincial to appoint him/her to this job." When the day comes that the individual religious can take the responsibility for jobs well done and for jobs poorly done, religious life will have endorsed the wise managerial strategy used in the business world. If a provincial could tell an appointee "Tell me what you need in order to do the job. If it's available, you'll have it. But after that you will be evaluated on your performance. You will stand or fall on what you do. If you fail, don't expect me to bail you out; if you succeed, all the credit is yours"—the issue of responsibility would have progressed far beyond what has been traditional. In the past we have heard such supportive statements as "Do the best you can."—"All I ask is that you try."—"Don't worry about the result."—"God will supply what is wanting." Clearly these are responsibility loopholes.

Yet another loophole for avoiding responsibility is to remove oneself from the vulnerable position of having to admit to an error of judgment by means of the expedient of denying the adequacy of the evidence presented in support of the judgment. This is at least occasionally seen in the rejection of a marginal member or in the decision to discontinue his/her membership in the congregation. This is sometimes accomplished by telling the members that "you really don't belong here" and "in fact, as far as can be determined you never did have a vocation here; it lies elsewhere". For the authors it seems impossible for any human being to be so certain of the action of the Holy Spirit. A superior or a community can clearly tell a person that he/she is not effective as a teacher, not competent as an administrator, not relating harmoniously within the community—but that is all that can be said. That might indeed mean that the religious in question does not fit into the announced goals and service of this particular congregation. But we cannot know that it means that the Holy Spirit has not moved that person to work out his/her invitation to sonship/daughtership *as a religious*. Again it seems somewhat contradictory that, for those religious who persevere, the accidents of history and circumstance which impelled that person to this particular congregation come to be accepted as obvious evidence of the pattern of operation of the Spirit while for those marginal people those same accidents of history are clearly outside the pale of the Spirit for "there never was a vocation".

The errors of judgment are errors at the human level of evaluation of quite human credentials. If the judgments allowed entrance to a person whose behavior is such that he/she is unable to carry out the particular form of the apostolate or to function effectively in other possible openings, that error of judgment has little to do directly with the action of the Spirit.

Human judgment and human intelligence will be obliged to confront a number of obstacles to significant movement or change in religious life. An honest address towards these difficulties will do much to speed the work of revitalizing religious life. It should be clear that the elimination of difficulties cannot carry the entire franchise for the renewal of religious life. Something more positive must be added. We see the double effort as concurrent so that both approaches need to be considered. The following list are some of the obstacles requiring attention if revitalization is to be undertaken:

    1. *A sense of personal isolation.* This is often one of the hidden dynamics underlying much of the behavior in religious life. This sense of isolation is usually an unverbalized reality that religious themselves refrain from discussing. Their hesitancy arises from a reluctance to admit to the possibility of personal failure in their quest

for that life-style in which they could experience and the world could see how "they love one another." Religious rarely share more personal beliefs and values with each other. Under these circumstances a sense of isolation is difficult to avoid.

2. *A lack of trust.* A sense of mistrust in religious life is far more prevalent than anyone would care to admit. This is not seen as an intrinsic defect of religious life but rather more directly is a consequence of poor communication between religious themselves. Only theoretically can one trust what one does not know. In our opinion there remain huge communication problems within religious life. These problems bring about skepticism, cynicism, rigidity of personal beliefs and evaluations which normally result in non-cooperation.

3. *Entrapment within years of habit and tradition.* An appeal is often made that this encapsulation both explains and exonerates oneself for the ideological stance taken on all matters concerning religious life. But such an argument is as defensible in explaining change as it is in explaining non-change. For it is true that some religious are the products of a relatively stable society and ethic in the recent past; and some are the products of our current unstable society. It follows that some religious are rooted in non-change and others are rooted in change. Therefore such encapsulation really explains very little unless the religious see themselves as non-thinking humans. Many religious refuse to look at the need for change; on the other hand, many refuse to look at the cost of change— along the human dimensions.

4. *A sense of personal insignificance.* In speaking to a person in religious life, only rarely will you note a sense of his/her personal significance. Most evaluations are of priests, Brothers or Sisters, of a priest, a Brother, a Sister, of our value to the Church, of our value to society. It is extremely difficult to catch any sense of one's personal

significance, for religious rarely speak of this priest, this Brother, my value. Perhaps this is because the measuring rods of significance seem to be productivity and accomplishment. Under the ethic that it is spiritually therapeutic never to speak of one's own contribution to the commonweal, religious fight feelings of personal significance lest they be courting the disaster of prideful behavior. They try to downplay their own significance, they try to disown their own accomplishments, they try to suppress the feelings of worth. Fortunately for many, they usually fail.

5. *Islands of security.* As subsidiarity and decentralization became more accepted and widespread, and as the individual's freedom to choose the type and site of his/her apostolic work became an experimental venture it was rather inevitable that enclaves of security would come to exist in various houses of many congregations. Having sought for, fought for and found a good thing, many religious settle down to modes of apostolic work which are not likely to change and which will tolerate little if any outside interference. Thus, while there may be more freedom to move within the perimeters of religious life, the evidence in many congregations is that there has been less movement of religious among existing houses of the congregation. One result of this reality is the weakening of any sense of corporate identification.

6. *Image maintenance.* Much of the effort of religious communities seems aimed at maintaining the proper expectations of the laity, either those presumed by religious life to exist in the mind of the laity or those actually operative in the laity, which exert a strong influence on the behavior in religious life. Indeed departures from answering fidelity to these expectations and to the ideals of the founder of the congregation are reprehensible beyond any possibility of being justifiable. Imputations of unfaithfulness, or of loss of the congregation's spirit, of

selfishness, of lack of concern for members of the congregation, of scandal to the surprised and shocked laity are readily heard. While the founder's inovative and creative vision is loudly applauded and due veneration granted for that reason, it seems that any thrust to follow such a lead by being similarly responsive to the Spirit is immediately and uncritically suspect. The coordinates of permissible behavior are well drawn and much energy on the part of those in religious life is spent making sure that they maintain behavior within those bounds so as to maintain the acceptable image.

7. *Intolerance*. Length of years in religious life can result in firmly entrenched personal convictions. And we can be glad that this is so. But they can also result in a devastating intolerance of those who do not share these convictions. The very outcomes that might be expected after years of daily Mass, meditation, spiritual reading, retreats—namely, more openness, more kindness, more understanding, more humility, more acceptance—seem to have escaped religious life in many instances. One could wonder if religious could prove that they had prayed so well for so long and so deeply.

Religious often initiate their efforts to reform, to renew or to change by limiting the sources from which they might gain insights as to the directions such efforts might or should take. The exchange of ideas with those who already share a marked similarity of thought and value is not likely to broaden perspective or to promote discovery of new areas of development. If religious listen only to themselves, then efforts to perfect their way of life can result in deformity. In such a situation perfective efforts have little relation to society as a whole, to history as a whole, to the Church as a whole. If those not within the ranks of religious life were to speak to religious, the religious might find out just to whom their life is of importance. The focus on the direction and substance of change might be thereby sharpened. One value of and one justification of religious life has been claimed to be its witness value. But to whom and to what does it witness? Most frequently the evidence of witness value comes from those already attuned to sharing the same value systems. In a sense, religious life witnesses unto itself. One can wonder what those with totally different value systems would say to religious life if they only had the invitation to speak to those in that life.

It becomes a poor argument to hold to the witness value of religious life when it appears currently that it is so weak in attracting members from its own constituency and when so many of its members, trained under the clear claim of witnessing to something of value, opt for some other way of living. Admittedly, religious life, properly conceived and honestly functioning, is witnessing to the reality of the Lord Jesus. And it has every right to ask its members to continue to give such witness even if there is no one reading it. If no one reads the life as having a witness impact, the sound of its witnessing is debatable. At the very least, religious life should not delude itself into the comfortable assumption that vast multitudes of humanity do see that life as witnessing to the Lord Jesus.

There are increasingly frequent signs that the public at large is withdrawing whatever concessions it has traditionally granted religious life as indeed different, as indeed witnessing to something. Tax exempt status is experiencing a constantly narrowing base. It can also be argued that the allocation of public funds in some form or other to the support of enterprises under the control of religious congregations is not in recognition of the witness value of such work but is rather an admission of the need for the continuance of such endeavors for the sake of the commonweal. The point being stressed here is that however true the witness value of religious life, it is no longer enjoying a clear pre-eminence in the scale of life-styles. Nor is it claimed that religious life could not again be a widely seen and accepted witness. At the moment it is not so viewed. In an increasingly pluralistic and socialistic world, more than ever there is the need for the faith response which holds that there is a tangible witness reality to religious life.

It is our view that strengthening the impact of religious life on the people of God in this day and age is dependent on listening attentively to those who clearly do not share the same value system, faith convictions and apostolic affiliations. That listening cannot be done from afar, from the isolation of our religious houses. Religious life must take the initiative to bring about the exchange.

The traditional apostolates of the majority of religious congregations had less to do, in their origins, with careful planning and intelligent foresight than they did with the historical accident of responding to the changing conditions of humanity and its needs. To this perception of existing circumstances, the founders of the various congregations added large measures of generosity and adaptability. The mobility and accommodation of religious of the twentieth century in responding to the needs of mankind are hindered to the degree to which the religious community identifies with its particular historical and accidental antecedents rather than with the more simple thrust of response to the suffering and needs of mankind in the present. Religious life which once lead in service, now, more often than not, follows. Perhaps this is indicative of a major shift in purpose for religious life. Perhaps religious life is no longer to be the breaker of new ground but rather the sustainer of ventures in which others lose hope, interest or commitment. Perhaps instead if witnessing to what men/women have not seen, it is to witness to what men/women saw and left when the going got too rough, or when the glory of discovery or initiation had waned.

We have seen the leadership role of religious life suffer an eclipse. Perhaps now it has a different function—a supportive, a substantiating, a living outside the limelight, an assuming of more obscure roles. It is here that the challenge to creativity can be seen for there is nothing more creative than to keep alive those values mankind has discovered and fostered in service to men and women. Creativity does not only mean to be out at the fringes of discovery. It can simply mean keeping a great and good thing viable, real, wholesome, functioning, contributing to mankind's fulness.

The endorsement of such an objective for contemporary religious life will not automatically resolve any major portion of its ills. To some, this objective will destine religious life to become circumscribed in a static position with little flexibility. To others, the objective is so valuable that resistance to encroachment becomes a focus of concern. To the first group, religious life would have difficulty demonstrating a dynamic quality if it foregoes an easily recognizable leadership role. It will be especially difficult for youth to accept this preservation objective despite the fact that their own goal of rejuvenating and restructuring their world is in essence a call to return to the very values that religious life endorses—however short of achieving the objectives it may be. Thus a tension is born between those who see the role of religious life to be preserver of the past ventures and lasting values and those who envision religious life as needing to be on the frontier of new apostolates, new leadership roles.

What is not at all certain is that it would be impossible for religious life to hold both objectives. If endorsement of one objective means the repudiation of the other, then more hard times lie ahead for religious life. If religious life was indeed a thing, was indeed substantive, in its own right, it might then be argued that such a society with two disparate objectives could not perdure. We shall have to stop reifying religious life if we want to escape the conclusion that under the impetus of change in the world it is destined to splinter or to be destroyed. Religious life is not a thing in itself. Yet we speak as though it is, going so far as to identify a Dominican religious life, a Carmelite religious life, a Trappist religious life, a Marist religious life, and so forth. The one thing that can bring about the demise of communities is the internal alienation of members from each other, resulting from conceptualizing religious life as a "given" with clearly defined objectives and unchangeable mode of living. This "it" posture is so behavioristic in its ethic that the word "life" seems a misnomer. Men and women banded together in religious societies in support of their already existing spiritual life with the expressed hope that the societal nature of these groupings would foster that very spiritual life. Further, as a small society they would be more effective in responding to the suffering and needs of mankind. However, efficiency of response is not the essence of religious life.

Maybe what is really needed for the revitalizing of religious life is to be convinced that God has no particular need for this particular community and its social expression though He is certainly concerned about the persons involved in it. Community should always be conscious of its very accidental (though providential) beginnings. One weakness in many attempts at revitalization is the triumphalistic attitude that religious have. They somehow come to feel that a particular community (their own) is indispensible. It often happens that the phase-out of the long-standing apostolic works barely disturbs the society in which these enterprises were functioning. Whatever concern is demonstrated is a concern at the level of the pragmatic considerations—cost increase, service deficit, etc. The concern is not over the issue of the disappearance of a very important entity in the operation of the Church. Nor does one hear such developments as being interpreted as an indication of the indispensability of the particular congregation. If it was read that way, it is likely that the congregation would be forced to considerations of how to revitalize its existence so as to be or become a good thing for its members and to keep that good thing operative in the Church.

Within the congregations themselves, a very real attitude held by the members constitutes a strong deterrent to revitalization. It is a personal individualized conviction that "no one else loves the religious life the way I do." Each religious becomes convinced that his/her perceptions, values, and beliefs are in total harmony with what ought to be. It becomes important and rather easy to defend this righteous position and to resist the "attacks" of the not-so-faithful other members who seem bent on changing things. The implication is that others do not care about religious life—that I care more than most—that my caring is focused on essentials—that I cannot put trust in the other religious. It would seem that the more adequate attitude to any reform would be to begin with the belief that everyone cares—then go on from there. No precluder of mistakes, this attitude would carry some promise of revitalization.

3

Obedience: With Broader Perspectives

OBEDIENCE HAS LONG BEEN and still is the cornerstone of religious life. It is stressed in formation programs as being at the heart of this way of life. It is viewed as one of the more demanding sacrifices that the individual is called to make upon entrance into religious life. Obedience is a difficult thing to accept since it seems to touch all those areas of our humanity that are so much our own and that go to compose our self-respect, our dignity. It touches our freedom, our free disposal of our existence; it touches our own sense of moral and intellectual capability to make a judgment on a situation; it touches our conscience, it touches the ability of a man or woman to risk.

Because obedience dares to contact so many areas of crucial concern to a man or to a woman as they engage in the work of being fully man or fully woman, it may be of greater significance in establishing the special nature of religious life than either celibacy or poverty. The focus of celibacy now is quite specific even though it does touch on a basic human right. Similarly the vow of poverty has a sharp focus. But obedience is very encompassing in what it affects in the day-to-day living of religious life. It is in the larger context of religious obedience that celibacy and poverty will come to be discussed as religious life addresses its own future.

It is obvious that obedience is rooted in a relationship of a person to another person. The latter may be another individual or a corporate person in a moral or civil sense. For this reason, it would seem that the better the explanation of the quality of the relationship, the better obedience would be understood.

For the Christian, obedience has its foundation in his/her total dependence on Christ. This dependence is called total since there was nothing that the Christian could do to attain what was accomplished in the suffering-death-resurrection of that Lord. Obedience then for the Christian will have the marks of the paradox to be found in that salvific act, the mark of losing one's life to find it, the mark of dying before one is truly alive, the unexplained paradox that mankind is saved through suffering and death—and through no other way.

Obedience as evangelical counsel is not something commanded by Christ but is something seen clearly in His life. That Christ is the model for obedience, especially religious obedience, is nothing new. But granting that be true, it would seem that obedience would have to be continually understood, corrected and amplified in terms of each new understanding of who this Christ is. As the Church comes to a deeper understanding of the mystery of the Incarnation, she is also broadening her understanding of obedience. Many of the problems in the Church and in religious life arise because we try to understand some things in themselves—without the continual effort to know our Christ better.

Some people feel that there would be little problem with obedience if they had to deal only with God. But this is wishful thinking because they just will not have that face-to-face confrontation in this life. Contact with God is normally a mediated contact. This mediated aspect of humanity's contact with God introduces all the vagaries of psychological functioning on the part of mankind. Even prayer is a psychological experience—though certainly it is not only a psychological experience. The admonition of Tillich to avoid the word "only" in writing theological treatises is also appropriately applied to psychology. The psychological equipment that human beings bring to the God-contacting experience does not vary essentially from person to person but there is nevertheless a sense in which the experience is unique. Uniqueness of a person which is something beyond similarity of psychological equipment immediately establishes uniqueness of experience. The temptation is strong to discuss obedience from the viewpoint of the unique experience of the individual person. But the Christian's problem (and also the problem for theology and psychology) is compounded by the fact that he/she is not only an individual but is also a member of a people.

Christian obedience has three dimensions. These are the example (and consequences) of the obedience of Jesus to the Father, the obedience of the People of God to that Lord, and then the obedience of Christians in service to each other. The exclusion of any dimension in the effort to understand obedience can only preclude a satisfactory understanding. There is an ordering in the importance of these dimensions; that ordering follows the dimensions as listed—from that of highest importance to that of lesser importance. It appears crucial to the proper perspective on obedience to see that the ordering extends from Christ, then to His people (as Church) and then to individuals. In the day-to-day life of the religious, the encountering of the demands of obedience tends to emphasize a reversed order of encountering. The immediacy of the person to person demand is the first experience. It is often the next step which is omitted for a transitional jump is made in by-passing the input that could be expected from the fidelity and faith of the People of God. The jump is made from the person-to-person reality directly to Christ's obedience to the Father as not to be comprehended or measured by human wisdom but at the same time to be the very model for our human obedience.

This by-pass has all the advantages accruing from efficiency of operation, from delineating clear lines of authority and obedience—from Christ to religious superior—to the individual religious, in validating on-the-spot commands as the inescapable mainfestation of God's will, in requesting a true faith-response from the individual. At the same time it introduces a hassle of other problems in the implied invitation to forget that the two people are two limited, fallible, reasoning, believing, thinking, hoping, planning, loving, fearing individuals. Since Christ did not grant the gift of inerrancy to either, a measure of wisdom and safety is to be found in paying attention to the insights of the collective faith of the People of God. When spiritual authority bespeaks the faith of the People of God (in their manifesting the obedience of Christ) it has validation and thus more easily secures compliance and acceptance. It is authoritative only when it adequately, honestly and truthfully expresses the faith of the people.

Part of the Christian's dependence on Christ is his submission as well to the Church of Christ, to its commandments and to those things which the Church delineates as bound up with salvation. The Church is an authority; it is the quality of the relationship between the believer and this authority that definitely affects obedience. Yet we must first remember that the main obedience for the Christian is the obedience of the Church to Christ, not of individual members to an authority. Here again the word "only" would be inappropriately included in either part of the preceding sentence.

The nature of relationship (any relationship) calls for development and growth on the part of both parties to that relationship. For a father to exact or expect the same style of obedience from his teenage son as he did when the son was in a less complicated time of life is to court the problem of rebellion. For if obedience is played out in a human relationship, then it is not just the rightness or wrongness of the demand (or expectation) for obedience but the style or quality of the relationship itself that will affect the response of the individual. Vatican II seems to be saying this when it uses so many humanly descriptive words when referring to our authority figures—loving father, caring shepherd, etc.

If the Church is to use Christ as example, then she must use the total complex of the obedience of Christ as example. That necessarily means and includes the quality of the relationship. God the Father did not just demand obedience to certain things but it was the "Who" and the "How" that were as important in the total complex that is Christ's obedience. While the gratuitous work of redemption could have been accomplished in any number of ways, there must be some special significance, some special import in how it was accomplished. The creator-created relationship (and the obedience required therein) was explicated by the total complex of Christ's obedience.

Our own human experience with obedience, whether to parents, to civil authority, to school authority, to religious authority, to Church authority, acknowledges the truth that problems with obedience do not often arise from what was commanded, but with the "why" or "lack of why," with the "timeliness" of what was commanded. These problems arise in a relational context. This implies that the burden of authority-obedience is shared by all involved, not just the subordinate. Obedience in contemporary religious life is as much a matter of relationship as it is of content. It is not efficiency alone which pressures authority-based organizations to move towards decentralization, subsidiarity, collegiality, small group living. Rather, men and women are coming to realize that obedience (respect for law and order, etc.) is really as dependent upon the quality of relationship as upon the command they are asked to obey. It is an open admission that obedience is bound up with the quality of relationships. The contributions of the field of developmental psychology concerning how the growing child acquires concepts and behaviors consonant with the requirement of obedience support this thesis of the importance of relationships.

The notion of the authority figure being the one and only channel through whom God's will is made known for the community or for the individual no longer has the potency it once had. In a paternalistic/maternalistic structure it might well have had meaning but as against collegiality and subsidiarity the notion finds sharply reduced acceptance. American religious, at least a significant number of them, are beginning to hold that the discerning of the will of God who is the Father of a people is best done by a people rather than by an individual. To discern God's will is something to which every Christian is bound. Salvation itself is based upon his/her response to this God.

The task of discerning the Spirit of God is not something that can be reduced to any governmental means of solving practical difficulties. It is not something that can be handled by a democratic model of decision making. Democracy fails for the reason that what is to be discerned is not man's/woman's spirit but God's and God's Spirit will not be fettered by democracy nor be contingent or subject to any other form of interpersonal compromise mankind might have developed. God could use the democratic process as a channel for manifesting His Spirit but what we must guard against is the claim that He invariably does use this channel. No governmental methodology or structure can claim that it is the one and only channel employed by the Spirit: that mode of governance must be chosen which offers the freest expression of the Spirit and which fosters listening and illumination. The mode need not be that which makes men/women most happy, but should be the one which allows for the greatest possible activity of the Spirit.

It cannot be totally argued that the discernment of the activity of the Spirit could not be accomplished by an individual. For prophecy is one of the charismatic gifts of the Church. However, for that prophetic insight to deeply affect mankind and its history, as the Spirit is wont, it needs the affirmation of a people. Prophetic activity is in service of a people, not of the individual. Unfortunately there have been and still are some religious afflicted with the "white knight" syndrome who fearlessly mount their charger to single-handedly change religious life.

That white knight will find two types of authority operative in religious life. One deals with the operation of a social structure and organization. Within this mode the position of authority and responsibility is indispensible. The limits of that authority are usually specified and are normally accompanied by procedures available to the electors for the removal of the individual who abuses authority or responsibility. Indeed no social organization can function effectively without there being some one individual responsible for the functioning of the organization. The quality of obedience to this function of authority is contingent on the human wisdom, acumen, creativity, administrative and other practical or intellectual abilities of the individual in that position of authority.

The second of the authority types, the spiritual authority, functions within a radically different framework. It is not of itself attached to any particular office of any particular organization. It is neither established or obliterated by any particular goverrmental procedure. Spiritual authority has validity when it speaks the Gospel and enjoins those who vow obedience to God to follow that Gospel. In those instances where authority is operative in areas other than those immediately consonant with the Gospel the authority is no longer spiritual in a strict sense. Within a community that has a religious base, the two functions of authority (the social and spiritual) can become confused in both the leader and the led. Within the organization framework of religious life, we cannot pattern the spiritual authority on the model of the spiritual authority as it exists in the Church.

Religious life, though indeed of benefit and even of necessity to the life of the Church, is not a miniature of the Church itself. As stated previously, religious life is accidental to Christ's Church. The authority within religious life is indeed true authority. But the model for those in authority in religious life would be more like the loving parent of a loving family.

The question of obedience is often treated in too static a fashion as applying to discrete little events. It is surely possible to place it in a larger context and to treat it as part of a process—a process directly related to the communal aspect of our shared sonship/daughtership. In the past, unquestioning obedience was seen to have a cumulative effect on the acquisition

of humility or abasement. To be sure, virtue by quantitative accretions is open to challenge. But the point made here is that the
cumulative effect had its reference point in the effect on the
individual religious. But acts of authority and of obedience have
a cumulative effect not just on the individual but also on the
community where they should rightly have that effect if we
really are a People of God.

Our human categories of response and categories of evaluation may have become too individualistically restrictive to allow
a full discernment of God's will for us. Perhaps this is precisely
what Christ is telling us in the story of the woman taken in
adultery. Maybe the appeal to law, right and just as it is, is
too restrictive in the possible categories of response to God's
will. Maybe obedience in discrete little events is not as important
as would be responses in other categories not always in awareness at a given moment. As Christ invited the person who was
without sin to cast the first stone He was inviting a shift in the
thinking the accusers. He was asking for a discernment of His
will which goes beyond the categories of judgment and evaluation written into law, written by humans so as to secure obedience
and conformity. Again it is not the right of society to legislate
that is disputed. It is the possibility that we have focused on
obedience in too narrow a fashion, in too individualistic a fashion.
Had a stone been cast, Christ would have to accept the justice
of the action but He would likely have regretted the apparent
limitations put on His own love and will for the people of God.
Christ wants us to see that He is not to be hedged in by our
human categories of judgment and evaluation. He invites us to
broaden our vision and our understanding of the ministry of
reconciliation which He has given us.

Obedience in a community of people becomes more difficult when that community is not quite certain as to what and
why it is. It is our conviction that each age has to come to a
restatement of its meaning, of its spirit. Very likely it will not
be vastly different in spirit from what it was in the past but

that spirit has to be regained, recaptured, restated in each age. People have to have a role in constituting the spirit they are going to live by. Thus each Christian tries to grasp the spirit of what it means to be a Christian. Though essentials may not be different from the spirit of the past (nor its devotions much different for that matter) yet each Christian will do something to make it his/her own. The engagement in this continual process makes for the vitality of Christian living. We tend to more readily give acquiescence and obedience to that we had a role in making.

It is that psychological truth which would argue for the value of allowing a group or community to discover (in the very process of interactive living) its own spirit rather than starting from *a priori* position as to how to create or build a community. One of the major obstacles to achieving genuine religious community is the very attempt to make or create it. A distinction is important here. If community means the reality circumstances in which interaction of human beings with each other can take place, then perhaps it is possible to create the optimal conditions for that interaction to take place. But propitious circumstances are not in themselves community for without people interacting there is no community. Real community has a spiritual dimension as its salient characteristic. George Orwell painted a word picture of a functioning group which most of us would hesitate to call a community. The love, trust, giving, suffering and receiving that are part of a true community are not things that can be legislated, planned or programmed by Orwell, provincial councils, or individual superiors. Community happens—usually when individuals have no preconceived notions about how it should be. They may well have some notions of what should be in community but remain open as to how these elements will be manifested. It is only in seeing the many different "hows" that a person comes to a better grasp of what he/she believes, feels, thinks, and loves. And having so arrived, he/she "lives" community.

Creating community often has the overtones of a mono-
lithic creation into which each individual must fit—usually requiring compliance with general functioning, laws, pre-set custom,
etc. But community does not mean conformity to externals; it
does mean living with like heart and with one Spirit which is
not ours; for the moment we want to register a concern about
pre-fabricating community. In our work with religious congregations across the country we have come to recognize the limited
number of categories which many congregations will accept or
tolerate as being possible areas where the Spirit can breathe.
Having breathed once, the Spirit must forever breathe within
the limiting coordinates of the system we human beings have
developed. Granted all the difficulties of discernment of the
Spirit, we may be fencing Him in by a priori judgments as to
where and how and when He will interact with us.

Though the Church will always have to be marked with
the lived example of the obedience of Christ, her members still
have to remember that they are a sinful people and must look
everywhere to find any assistance to help them to do better in
what they have been called to do—to be like Him. Here we
can (or perhaps must) look at what "secular" man has discovered about obedience and how he has tried to solve that
problem. For like it or not, though we are living a grace life,
what goes on in that secular world affects what goes on in the
Church.

Obedience is best elicited in that situation, in that relationship, where the individual has had a real role in the shaping
of the relationship. Packaged situations and packaged relationships do little for the cause of obedience. An active role in the
structuring of both is essential. Our God does this in dealing
with us. Though He has given certain things for our obedient
acceptance, He has left it up to us as to how we will concretize
them. For instance, He has said I must love my brother/sister
the way He did. I look at Him and see that He served, that
He suffered, that He healed, that He forgave, that He was

reconciled, that He died for that brother/sister. But how I will concretize all those things in my life and in this age is left up to me. In effect I am obedient to a style of life but not to concrete specifications of that life. I must enter the sphere of broader categories of response rather than attempt to focus on discrete little events. Such discrete models are not behavior models but were intended to be category models waiting upon my personal implementation within the context of the circumstances of my life.

In endorsing obedience to a style of life rather than to a list of things commanded, we have to address the question of whether or not there is a hierarchy to be established in the things commanded. We are hard put to find any hierarchical ordering in the life of Christ beyond the clear mandate to love God and my neighbor as I do myself. Thus any behavior motivated by genuine love defies ordering. Yet because of our humanity, because we are still a sinful people, though redeemed, we find it convenient to install a hierarchy of actions in terms of social expediency, in terms of the realization of a social goal, in terms of achieving the objectives of institutional commitments. What must be realized is that these orderings have their origin in our own human condition—not in any *a priori* categories of response set down by Christ.

In His wisdom, Christ did not communicate any principles for discerning God's spirit. Thus the traditional concept of religious obedience as being an incontestable channel for the revealing of God's Will is not based on solid theology. This is not to dispute the value of that faith response which may prompt men and women in religious life to accept obedience as a concretization of their own free choice to live a life style close to the invitation extended by Christ. But it does say that there might be a touch of arrogance in trying to decide how God's will is to be made manifest. It is quite audacious for any person to say that he/she speaks the voice of God. The subtle overextension of promised infallibility fails to accept the fact that

Christ's promise was not a promise to risk nothing fallible. It was a promise, a determination, to control the fallibility of His Church.

Religious obedience that bases its ascetical or perfective efficacy on the view that God's will is incontestably made manifest through the commands of superiors is in for rough times. In the realities of daily living, the further we get from the fundamentals, from the essentials of obdience to God, to His Will, the greater effort is exerted to convince the obeying religious that what is commanded is commanded in God's Will. Obedience comes to be required and demanded simply because one constituted in a position of authority has delivered a command. Such approaches are seen in family life and in religious life. Partial justification might be granted in the case of a parent dealing with immature, unreasoning, unmotivated child. But the religious life scene hardly plays with these types of *dramatis personnae*.

The strong tide of movement towards subsidiarity and particularly towards collegiality weakens the strength of the argument that God's Will is made manifest throught the decisions of a religious superior. For it is indeed possible that a superior holds a view or a position clearly in opposition to the collegially derived stance of a religious community. It is very doubtful that the religious will resolve such a dilemma without considerable anguish in view of the firm hold that tradition and insistent teaching have on his/her own concept of religious obedience. Part of this anguish has its source in the fact that collegiality involves personal participation and personal responsibility. Even though involvement on the part of the individual is participatory, it does move the participant a bit closer to the position that his/her judgments will be part of the effort to discern the movement of the Spirit in the affairs of the community. This heightens the sense of responsibility; this may augment a feeling of anxiety. One could allay this anxiety by adhering to the traditional view of obedience. But difficulties arise from the fact that being sure of God's Will is not the only psychologically desirable state of affairs weighing in on our humanity. Certainty as to the way one should behave may be no more conducive to growth and development than uncertainty with its constant element of search.

A strong case in support of obedience in religious life can be made from considering the nature of the social organization which religious life surely is. Whenever people band together to work at a common social goal there is need for organization authority. If a community commits itself to some job, to some social work entirely under its own jurisdiction, then the community must recognize and accept the need for lines of authority—unless it judges its enterprise to be totally different from all other human social undertakings. Religious life, or rather those living that life, unnecessarily complicate the problem of obedience by failing to maintain the differentiation between the work of the congregation and the state of life of which religious life is but one type. Each religious is to be expected as a mature individual to operate in such fashion as to meet life's decisions in a way which seems to be prudent and informed to him/her. It follows that with many such prudential judgments offered by the many members of the community, the need for an authority becomes more insistent. Religious obedience is necessary in order to overcome the inertia which would result from competing prudential judgments. There could be a variety of ways in which that authority is established—election, appointment, consensus, majority vote, control by an elected board, etc. While the manner of exercising authority is not unimportant, for the present discussion it is the need for authority which is advocated. This need is based not on any religious or spiritual life principle but on the need for efficiency in the operation of a social organization. While some religious may be dissatisfied with this orientation because it seems to minimize the spiritual aspects of obedience, their lack of enthusiasm in no way negates the reality of their membership in social organization. If over and above this sociological necessity for authority (and hence obedience) the religious want to inject a faith-response to authority, they have every right to do so.

It is quite possible that the prudential judgment of a religious superior be less prudent, less informed, less wise than the judgment of a member of the community. No promise of inerrancy was ever given to any person who happens to occupy a certain position in religious life. Some judgments of men/ women as superiors are poor ones, some have caused the loss of considerable financial resources in the history of religious congregations. If one could argue with any degree of certitude that such calamitous decisions were in accord with God's Will, it would be a demand for renunciation of another of His gifts— human intelligence. Yet in the face of this poor decision by the superior, the religious would have to act in accord with it— after diligent efforts to secure a change of decision—simply because there is authority acting. It would not necessarily be a case where the Will of God has been made manifest. Rather it is the nature of the social organization which requires compliance or, in an extreme, loyal opposition. But it should be clear that such a view of religious obedience shifts the focus and responsibility to the individual religious and away from the superior. The religious must learn to accept, even when disagreeing, the decisions of authority in the social scheme of religious life. But there must also be developed ways and means for removing from authority positions those whose judgments and decisions are detrimental to achieving the social objectives of the community and whose relations with the community in the sphere of life or living, apart from social goals, are quite poor.

Decisions at the level of the social service function, easily invite the concurrence of intelligent religious—at least as to the necessity for decisions of this type. Decisions which affect personal life styles (again apart from the social service goal) are less readily accepted. The sweep of the changes in the world today gives rise to pressures affecting the personal life styles of religious. Much of their behavior has been limited by non-involvement with those not within religious life. There is no opportunity for marriage and therefore no sexual relations with others. But presently the question as to how religious life is to be positively related to others is being asked more and more frequently. And apparently there are no longer any predetermined answers handed down by authority for the effort to discover an answer involves the personal life style of the individual. The pursuit of an answer involves but goes beyond the social service function of the community. This social involvement places certain limitations on the development of life style—if one wants to maintain membership. Authority invoked in the pursuit of the social goal of a community remains something different than authority invoked to influence personal life styles of the members. Admittedly, the line of demarcation is a difficult one to draw.

One of the sanctioned motives for entering religious life has always been to save one's soul. One could hardly quarrel with that desirability. However under current emphasis we are coming to understand that we are saved not merely as individuals without mutual bonds and ties to others but that our salvation is intimately related to Christ's wish that we become a single people. This clearly involves a vast world of reciprocal relationships with the People of God. A thesis could be advanced that much of the relating between religious and laity has been predominately a one-directional relationship initiated, maintained and fostered by the laity. As things turned out, much attention was given by religious and by the laity to those features about religious life which were judged to be of high value. Religious transmitted a monastic spirituality to the laity without much thought as to its applicability or appropriateness. How many young Christians felt guilty at failing to say their morning and evening prayers! As long as religious life either promoted or tolerated the pedestal approach by the laity, it was difficult to develop interrelationships. In the cause of sanctity, religious Sisters willingly taught almost gratis; the laity came to accept this as part of the dedication of the Sisters despite the reality factors of existing economic conditions. Because of this and many other behaviors, it became assumed that religious do not need many of life's compensations as do the laity. Religious life tended to foster this assumption in support of a praiseworthy image of asceticism.

Many of these assumptions and beliefs are now subject to open, honest investigation. To the ultimate benefit of all concerned, such openness is necessary since the problems of contemporary religious life are not solvable in a relationship vacuum. Problems in one area are not solvable without adjustments in the other. The basic premise for this position arises from the truth, time-honored and preached, that the source of religious vocation is the Christian family. What that family believes about religious life, how that family interrelates with members of religious congregations, what evaluations it places on the activity of the congregation and the behavior of its members are critical determinants of the future of religious life. As long as there is an isolation factor operating between laity and religious, especially in view of contemporary conditions of life, the prospect of renewed growth and development in religious life will remain slim. Not only must some windows be opened but some doors too—at least in the cause of occasional sharing. Both religious and laity must make their reciprocal relationships come into awareness. We are destined to be one people; we depend on each other. For all Christians, religious and laity alike, life is specified for them through baptism, to live as part of a people, to share in Eucharist, to pray, to be responsible to the evangelical counsels. The baptismal specification is universal in that it embraces all Christians. But we can go beyond that Christian membership—and indeed we must go beyond it. There was, prior to the specificity placed on Christians by baptism, the universal call to all to sonship/daughtership of the Father. Thus from either vantage point, religious life and the laity cannot justify an isolationist mentality —even though there can be respect for obvious differences.

Past isolationist practices are not discussed here in any judgmental sense but merely as historical reality. It is our developing understanding of Christ's message that invites new cooperation, collaboration, relationships among all of us human beings as the one People of God.

Thus there are two concepts, growing in potency within religious life, that forecast new understanding of religious obedience. One is the acceptance of a common sonship/daughtership, a People of God view of others. The more emphasis or focus given to this concept, the more the differentiating characteristics between laity and religious are minimized. Thus whenever the commands of religious obedience seem to be isolating religious from the People of God, they will come under challenge by those who have a strong sense of unity under the People of God concept. While it will always be incumbent on such religious to concede the necessity for rules and regulations for their social organization, the claim that such regulations are justified because they are spiritually perfective will not find ready acceptance. The great necessity in religious life today is the willingness to "call it as it is." What is proposed here is the admission that the endorsement of the communalities between religious and laity will have an effect on the practice of religious obedience. At a minimum, any regulation efforts, hoisted to the level of religious obedience, which tend to entrench basic differences between religious and laity are in for rough times.

The second concept forecasting new developments in our understanding of religious obedience is the problem and the reality of the Spirit operating in us humans as He decides. Whether we use such a term as "movement or discernment of the Spirit" or the term "charism," we are confronted with new challenges to religious obedience. Perhaps it would be better said that we face the task of reformulating our concept of obedience. Gone is the view that the Spirit is constrained to act only (there is that word again) through the activities of the religious superior. This clearly does not remove the possibility of God so acting but the openness to new avenues through

which the Spirit might act broadens the base for religious o-
bedience rather than narrows it. We cannot put restrictive
categories of action of the Spirit nor on our response to His
action. Yet we have to make some sort of judgment and decision
regarding areas of our free personal response. Lest it appears
that a heavy indictment is directed at traditional life, it should
be admitted that there was always acceptance and agreement
that the Spirit might be acting in special ways with regard to
religious life. For example, the broad scope and encouragement
given to the function of the spiritual director, the confessor,
attests to the willingness to accept this as a preferred channel for
the action of the Spirit. What has undergone change is the
dependence on the wisdom and insight of one person, the
spiritual director, as required prior to the response to the action
of the Spirit. Obviously, this change is not without the great
possibility of self-deception but it is nonetheless a change. It
seeks to safeguard itself against deception by reliance on the
activity of a people rather than on the one person. To illustrate
this point, it has long been recognized that social injustice is a
reprehensible thing. But perhaps it can be said that it took a
people, the various minority groups, to so shout this truth that
the conscience of other groups was roused from lethargy to
an insistent awareness of the problem. To many, the action of
the Spirit is obvious in the agitation by the minority groups.
Loud and clear was He announcing that mankind had forgotten
one of Christ's important truths, that we are our brother's
keeper.

It is and will remain a challenge as to how to discern
the action of the Spirit in the world today. Humorously but
not without a large measure of truth, one religious superior
described his current job as "coordinator of the varied charisms
of the members of the community."

4

Chastity: An
Affirmation of Humanity

ONE OF THE FIRST FEATURES about chastity that strikes anyone who directs attention to it is that those in religious life go at it as a profession and that the laity do not. But all men and women (not just those in religious life) are called to the evangelical counsels, it follows that there must be something more to chastity for the religious. It is something more but not something different. St. Paul's words to the Ephesians, speaking of what would look like a status difference between employers and slaves, are appropriate here. "... remembering that they and you have the same Master in heaven and He is not impressed by one person more than another" (Ep. 6:9). The value of the celibate state is not rooted in an intrinsic status difference. Its value is in terms of what it provides opportunity for, in terms of the type of work it provides and facilitates.

First off, it would appear that the celibate life is a more efficient way of trying to reach God. This does not argue that every celibate is effectively utilizing this means. With a person's ultimate destiny being union with God, it is likely that the more specified the one-to-one relationship, the better is that way to reach God. It is a question of means; it is a matter of personal choice in responding to Christ's call to chastity. There are different manners in which the counsel to chastity can be witnessed to. It is perhaps an infelicitous choice of words which emphasizes a "vow of chastity" as differentiating religious life from other states of life. All human beings without exception must be chaste. Vowing to be chaste is vowing to do what one ought to do in the first place. Vowing to be celibate is exercising a free option of the part of the person. There is no mandate to be celibate.

So often this vow is spoken of in terms of what it is not, terms which indicate what is not permitted to those who take this vow. It is more difficult to speak in positive terms about what it is. It is our belief that its true meaning can only be found in a greater understanding of the consequences of the Incarnation. The action of God in becoming man gave a value to humanity that it never had of its own. And from that moment on, the way to reach or go to Christ is through one's own humanity. Christ would have us understand that chastity has to do with much more than the sexual component and the affective component of human nature. Chastity is as much a command to use as it is a command not to abuse. The Christian must use his/her humanity as an avenue to reach Christ.

Chastity says something about a person's relationship to God only to the degree that it says something about relationships of person-to-person. If our love of God is purchased only at the expense of our love for men and women, then chastity has failed as a means. Long before the issue of vocational choice confronts the individual, that person has to confront the issue of chastity, for he/she does have a body. The issue of chastity is therefore prior to vocational state of life. It must therefore have something to do with the totality of our humanity. It involves the relationship of self to one's own body and the relationship to others as body. Part of the task of reaching integrated personhood requires the adequate development of these relationships. We are being called to integral psychological relationships because the God we are being called to is human, is Man. We are being called to union with Christ in full view of, not in spite of, our humanity.

Religious must and do witness the mystery of Christ by their celibate life. They witness to His purity through the non-use and non-abuse of their body in sexual activity. The witness value of this dedication is obvious and is good. The full understanding of the witness role requires the perspective arising from important prior realities. There is first of all the fact that Christ was like us in all things save sin. He therefore was very much a sexual person. Then there is another fact that He is alive still as man. These realizations and this faith should make it clear that the witness role in question cannot be to the mystery of Christ prior to the resurrection. That Jesus did not marry is important to our faith. But Jesus as the unmarried person is not the main or even substantiating reason for the celibacy of religious. To place celibacy at that level is to visualize Christ's life as rather negative. The witness value of this apparent non-involvement is not purchased at the cost of withdrawal from mankind. Jesus did not purchase His purity by removing himself from men and women but rather by being involved with them. Further, the resurrection affirms for humanity the active presence of Christ, as a man, fully man, with manhood purchased not by simple negation but by the affirmation of his humanity—an affirmation repeated in word and deed over and over again in Gospel accounts. The vitality, the saving presence of celibacy among us human beings can only be provided when the religious can couple his/her negation with the positive affirmation of self and of other human beings. There can be no positive affirmation of others without the prior affirmation of oneself. The religious cannot lay valid claim to the eschatological witness value of celibacy without making that witness a meaningful affirmation of their sexuality in this world.

One of the authors has been on the scene at a Catholic college that has gone through the experience of becoming a co-ed institution. Pertinent to the present discussion is the observation voiced by many of the undergrads that a sizeable number of the male faculty, particularly the male religious, are afraid of female students. Apart from the possibility of a misreading of professional academic behavior, there are some germane doubts about the scope of the witnessing desired by the religious in living their celibate life if the witnessing is read as the undergrads did read it.

It is the choice and subsequently the obligation of religious to witness to as much of the mystery of Christ as one can at any one time. This is what those in religious life strive to do. What we see happening is the opening up of new possibilities for witnessing . It is common knowledge that modern psychology is engaged in exploring numerous dimensions of human relationships, in citing many more aspects of relational possibilities. The list of avenues of these explorations is lengthy—T-groups, encounter groups, growth groups, consciousness raising groups, assertive training groups—to name but a few. And it is no longer a secret that new relationships among religious and new relationships between religious and lay folk grow and develop on the campus of universities when the religious are away from their usual surroundings. Such developments cause concern "back at the ranch." This concern in some quarters has reached the point of proscribing attendance at certain universities and colleges, of setting up competing programs of study in the greatly controlled environments of seminaries or houses of religious formation. It seems that there is a mixed bag of motives underlying these moves to structure the environment. Certainly it does not say much for the estimate of the maturity of American religious who as adults of twenty-five or more years are judged incapable of relating to others "as religious should"—whatever that term might mean.

The fear of scandal also prompts these decisions. Such fear cannot be dismissed by a simple *fiat*. It is a real concern in religious life and will remain operative as long as relations between sexes have a dominant sexual perspective. Treatises from the pens of psychologists are not likely to alter this perspective very much. Two things may help: a plumbing of the meaning of Christ's demand that we love the way He loved and the examples of wholesome relationships while maintaining commitment to religious life.

The universal call to chastity is a call to psychological integrity but not that alone. The role and function of grace will certainly affect relating. Often by default we fail to concede to the action of grace the efficacy that it can have in shaping human relationships. Further, the instruction of Christ adds a new dimension to relationships. He did not say: "Love one another." He did say: "Love one another the way I have loved you." This is a call to being human in a very specific way—that we love the way He loved. Yet there is something here over and above human potential—that something being the action of grace. For religious, as for all mankind, it becomes the task of continuing personal and communal discovery of what it means to love as Christ loved.

The source of understanding what Christ meant by His statement on love includes but goes beyond the Gospel. History attests to the fact that the Church has not limited her understanding of Christ's mandate to the words of the Gospel for she would be hard pressed to explain, by the Gospel alone, some of the stances she took that are matters of historical record—for example, the Huguenots, her treatment of heretics, the lack of social conscience except in selected areas like the care of the sick, the aged, the orphans. While the Christian can never dismiss the Gospels, he/she must come to accept the reality that Christ is alive in the present and speaks to the Church through the environment of social life. Therein must we explore how the loving as Christ loved is to be lived out. This can be done only by a continuing reappraisal of what we have come to know about ourselves. It is here that psychology can make the contribution.

Chastity was one of Christ's ways of loving. As one way, it can, of course be recommended and followed. It is however not the only way in which Christ loved. In our day the notion of chastity must be continually reappraised in terms of everything that human knowledge has uncovered as true about man, about woman. This was the essential note of Christ's life—that He loved to the total depth of what humanity is. It is our faith affirmation that He had perfect humanity and that it was the living out of that that was redeeming. Whatever science can show to be an authentic part of humanity must be integrated into our understanding of what it means to love as Christ loved. Christ desires to share life, His human life, in its totality with all mankind. To share one's life with others requires a great deal of trust. To share one's life with a selected few individuals is easier than to share it with all the People of God. It may be true that in the face of the frightful demands placed on religious in their sincere effort and desire to share life with others, they erect boundaries to the demands by carefully defining the group with whom the sharing will go on. This makes sense psychologically but it might be minimizing the full intent of Christ's invitation to share with all men. To take Christ at His word is always an awesome thing. The very rules and regulations in religious life have the effect of reducing opportunities for sharing save but with the members of a particular community. Yet the call to face the reconciling People of God is more direct and obvious in religious life than in other states of life. The membership is expected to take Christ's invitation and mandate very seriously—perhaps more intently than should be expected by those in other states of life. Only the grace of God can enable men and women to see something more in the People of God than a faceless crowd threatening an alienation.

The focus of sharing for those in religious life turns quite easily to a determination to share "things," to share in a common apostolate, to share in praying. There is always a hesitancy to share the more personal dimensions of one's being—a hesitancy which we are willing to say is more pronounced within the religious life than outside of it. This is unavoidable if sharing on the personal dimensions of life received a de-emphasis in training years and a reinforcement coming from years of persuasion that common observance of rule and custom was a primary goal of religious life. Very quietly the thesis of "person equivalence" took roots in religious life, nurtured by the claim to be good asceticism.

With a reluctant admission that it might not—just might not—be possible to love all persons equally or in the same manner, the tenets of religious life seem in the main to hold to the theoretical possibility that this faceless relating can be brought off equally. At least it is a goal to be striven for. Thus the "other"—the object of love—is like all "others"—to be loved equally. Yet one's subjective human reaction to being loved as yet another "other" fights this person equivalence approach to human relationships. Outside of the arenas of political and economic power, the most powerful people the world has known are those who seem to be able to personalize their caring about others. For their caring is not a cause to be achieved by life's end, not an objective to be realized at some point in time. They simply live their caring day-by-day, continually. Arguing here that the basic issue in considerations of chastity is that of the quality of relationships, we are immediately confronted with the reality of a language impoverishment which practically denies us the possibility of discussing these relationships. Sharing life is an aspect of personhood and is better understood in an actual experience of sharing than in reading treatises about sharing.

Perhaps there can be an argument made to support the contention that is easier to focus on events and things than on relational possibilities in religious life. Even in modern theological and spiritual writings we see shifts of focus that sometimes startle us or jar us into considering new avenues of understanding. For many months the popular reference language had us see the Eucharist as a celebration. As a celebration, attention was focused on a daily event, the daily happening of this celebration. Yet the first occasion when the Eucharist was offered to mankind, if we accurately assess the words of Scripture, had as much of the aspect of a sharing as it did a celebration. The whole of Christ's approach to Holy Thursday emphasized the sharing rather than an eagerness for a festive celebration.

But in religious life the emphasis has been on the Eucharist as a celebration, as the most important event or happening in the day of the religious. Thus being present for this event becomes a criterion for the full living of the religious life. The Church herself slipped into this celebration mentality with the multiple Masses on certain days of the year for her priests. The laity got caught up in this sanctity by numbers routine to some extent. It is not to decry nor denigrate the sincerity of those who choose to relate to God in these events, but it does seem healthy that the Church and religious are open to new possibilities of focus on the import of Christ's message to us.

The extreme difficulty encountered in any attempt to speak about sharing in a relational context seems very adequately epitomized in the words Christ chose to express the incomprehensible, the most profound sharing known to mankind—Christ sharing all that He is with us by giving us His body and blood. The words of this giving are simple, surfacely obvious, frightening from a human reading but of the essence of God's desired relationship with us.

After a period of heavy emphasis on the necessity of sharing in religious life, after a spate of testings in the semi-public arena of sensitivity or encounter groups, there has been a backlash of opposition to any accentuation of this aspect of life in religion. The baby risks being tossed out with the cooled waters of the bath. One result of the backlash of reaction is the muting of all attempts to speak of human relationships within religious life. The hesitancy to speak of such matters goes even as far as labeling the protagonists of this need to share as being "religious on the way out." The interpretation is that these religious are advocating something impossible to achieve in religious life. It may be worthwhile to explore the validity of such an interpretation.

The life style for religious life in these days is to be based on the knowledge and acceptance of the truth of our being first loved by God and by people thereafter. The time sequence of these events is not open to challenge. But in one's personal life, the learning to love and the learning about love do not follow the same chronicity. The human being does not attest to his/her being loved by God until he/she first comes to know what the word love itself means. And that knowledge is mediated only by other human beings.

The religious who tries to verify his/her celibacy in a direct one-to-one relationship with God has inverted Scripture somewhat. As John says: "No one can say he loves God unless he first loves his brother." If, therefore, celibacy is to say something about mankind's love of God, it must first say something about his/her relationship to others and to self. Only as these human relationships are clarified will a person's relationship with God take on its proper meaning. Celibacy says something about how human beings should be to each other—not how they should be to God. A religious does not relate to God as a celibate any more than a man relates to God as a husband or a woman relates as wife. The celibate status, the wife status, the husband status—all have to do with relationships among men and women, not with relationship to God. Only when I clarify my relations to my brother/sister will I understand how it is I must be to God since I will be to God only through my brother/sister.

As religious life has come to address this aspect of truth, there has been a shift of emphasis away from the voluntaristic approach to events and happenings. Based on faith this voluntaristic approach is a personal willing and choosing to respond more fully to God. It seeks to establish a one-to-one relationship and consequently secondarizes the element of human relationships. It is a truth of our humanity that we cannot love what we do not know and if we are charged with the necessity to love our brother/sister as we love ourselves it follows that a marked degree of self-confrontation and self-acceptance are to be very much a part of our relationship with God and His people. And no one comes to know himself at any level without deep interaction with others, without sharing what is deepest in him, without running the risk of disclosure, and even the risk of making mistakes. Celibacy, dealing, in our view, with the mode and quality of human relationships, is not to be had by fiat, not by pronouncing a vow in itself. It is to be had or, more properly, to be acquired by one's having matured precisely in those situational contexts in which sexual maturity is to be attained. Celibacy, in our view, is not a state; it is a mode of relating, a process to be entered into, a task of coming to know oneself in relation to other men and women.

Much, perhaps too much, of the self-awareness of those in religious life is destined to be the deceptive type of awareness which has its origin in a comparison of one's present status over against the model of holiness delineated in so many spiritual conferences in the training years. It is against the backdrop of what the religious "ought to be" that the effort is made to assess what religious really are. It is the end product of years of questing that is held up as the criterion against which religious are asked to evaluate self. The developmental aspect of the spiritual life and of the religious life receives little emphasis or attention. It is very difficult to present a carefully paced set of guidelines for development to young religious. The model is an "all-or-none" personification of what religious—all religious —should be.

The fallacy in the presentation of an ideal model of a religious is that this ideal never existed. For the model is usually a conceptualization of what "the" perfect religious should be. But in an accurate and strict sense, neither "religious life" nor a "religious" exist in this world of ours. This person or that person, each living a deeply spiritual life do exist. They euphemistically apply the words "religious" and "religious life" to themselves and to the conglomerate of life-style features which differentiate them from their brothers and sisters. Religious life has suffered as much from its own hagiography as sainthood has in the Church. Religious life has so many abstractions, conceptualizations and idealizations pervading its imperatives as to what its members should be that it is difficult to find the realities—at least the realities where a simple sinner can find a place. After Christ, our one image, if any religious is worth his/her salt, it is only because in his/her time, under his/her circumstances, in his/her situation, with his/her faults and gifts, he/she was able to present some witness to the world. But the word is *some* witness. It might also be possible that he/she caused difficulty for a great number of people either because of his/her holiness or the lack of it.

If there is an ideal image of the religious life which is to be held up for duplication by an aspiring religious, then we, in effect, move toward a negation of the possibility of God's Spirit working uniquely in him/her. The categories of response to the Spirit seem already determined by the model. Perhaps for that reason religious seem totally unopen to surprise; they take themselves too seriously; they work so assiduously to match the model that they leave no room for humor about the way the Spirit will work among men and women. Ideal images are indeed built upon the past and are often closed to the future.

Hidden below the triteness of acknowledging that the Church and religious life are caught up in the rapid changes of our unstable world there is shock and surprise over how the Spirit could have determined to "play his cards" differently than in the past. Church and religious life seemed to believe that the Spirit could be controlled and cajoled into following patterns of the past. What Church and religious life failed to note in their backward glances was just how surprising the Spirit really was. Thank God for a God who is neither a religious, a theologian, a psychologist, nor a Roman Catholic!

The sense of discovery, the sense of adventure, the sense of openness seem to be missing from the life of many religious. Though it can be conceded that many religious have honest and sincere motivation much of their early effort in religious life is imitation behavior. Heroic efforts are made to make the grand leap into the life of a genuine sanctity. Smiles of embarrassment often cross the face of religious as they reread some of their jottings from their early years of religious life. Most of them hasten to destroy these early testimonials to their own sanctity. For they see themselves now as still questing to reach such high degrees of holiness.

This understandable but somewhat unrealistic inversion of the full Christian life may constitute a genuine loss of opportunity. Many religious acknowledge that they are a long way from achieving the levels to which they aspired in early years. Life is seen as backsliding or as misdirected in having a set of unrealistic goals. Living under the imperative of what one "ought to be" may be less effective in reaching that very goal than living under the full awareness of what one is. For the reality orientation of what one is includes all that is to be subsumed under that very word "reality." It includes God, Christ, grace, Church, life, others. It need not be seen as an egocentric me-first approach to life. It injects the person into the stream of reality—the core of which might be caught in the use of such phrases as "the Spirit, now"; "God, now"; "grace, now"; "me, now in my totality"; "salvation, now." It is a focus on the present as being the only reality component over which the religious can exercise control now. It steers away from that attitude towards life which constantly reminds the person to so live that he/she may eventually get to heaven. There is no pie in the sky attitude that has a motivational potency that a reality orientation can't match or exceed.

A major component of love is the intention to give, to sacrifice, to willingly deprive oneself of any emphasis on the ego-serving return of love. Yet if one has the intention only to give, the authenticity of the love can be challenged. It may indeed be a way to avoid facing one's own self. The life style of the person who lives genuinely is not primarily earmarked by a voluntaristic approach (a willing to give) but is based on the knowledge and on the acceptance of being loved by God first and by people thereafter.

The achieving of this acceptance runs into some special obstacles in religious life. It is directly tied to what has been traditionally believed about the nature of vocational decision. Up to the present, the decision to enter religious life was invested with more "accomplished facts" than is justified. The vocational decision is appropriately made by a young person anywhere within the year span of twelve to twenty—following Ericson's developmental schema. But the personal acceptance of God's love of oneself and of another's love of oneself waits upon our working through the normal travail of the period of intimacy—as Ericson calls it. Except in a voluntaristic way, it is very difficult to make the decision about sharing love, sharing one's psychological self with another person if one has not confronted the intimacy struggle. Religious life accepts the validity of the vocational decision (and rightly so) but then builds a style of life which rather effectively precludes the resolution of the intimacy struggle. This preclusion acquires apparent justification in the assumption that acceptance of vocation is *the* important option for the individual human being. Any other choice is freighted with the implication of "non-cooperation with God's grace" or "failure." Having exercised that option, the newly accepted religious finds that other normal developmental challenges recede to an inconsequential status or into the limbo of challenges which religious life does not know how to deal with. Religious life in the early formation years has the tendency to foreclose the normal intimacy struggle long before the period of life when the resolution of that challenge is usually accomplished.

Until such time as religious life incorporates the normal developmental route and time schedule for growth into its formation programs we can expect a continuing exodus of religious who, after a number of years in the system, then opt for a different way of life where intimacy resolution seems more probable. The problem is not exclusively physical or sexual but is rather broadly concerned with the gratifications possible in family life. This is not to argue that religious life, differently conceived and structured, would be incapable of offering adequate opportunity for the resolution of the intimacy struggle. Nor is it claimed that none of the present day religious have been able to resolve the struggle. It is that the system is not conducive to resolution.

What is particularly detrimental to religious life is an ersatz resolution. This is the voluntaristic approach which persuades religious to care, to love, because "I ought to." "Religious ought to be loving people and therefore I will care because it is my duty. I would not be a good religious unless I cared about others." This begets an aura of toleration, a "saintly sacrificing of self" so as to serve the other. This approach uses the other for the purpose of propelling self further along the sanctity road. It is our thesis that this can and does happen very frequently because the intimacy struggle has not been worked through. Nothing more devastating to a human being is likely to happen than awakening to the realization that he/she is "loved" or "cared for" only because the other person operates from a duty imperative.

If religious life forecloses on the resolution of the intimacy struggle during the teens and twenties, it will come to see some of its members retreating to adolescent behavior later in life as they come to grips with the struggle. However late it occurs, typical adolescent reactions will be manifest. This is regrettable and often issues forth in further antagonisms in community living.

We are not here endorsing a position that the training years ought to provide opportunity for "testing" the vocational choice by experiences and contacts not usually associated with the training years. No call is made for more socialization as a "test" of vocation. Rather a call is made to reconsider training programs in terms of the high desirability to resolve the intimacy struggle prior to accepting the demands of the celibate life— not after acceptance. The need for a wide range of social relationships would be viewed as "testing the vocation" only if one lumps vocational choice and human developmental sequences under the one title of an all-at-once fact of one's individual life. The choice for religious life can be made validly before other developmental phases have been gone through—but gone through they must be. The attempt to bypass any phase will likely fail and produce plastic religious. They will be men and women who resolved the vocational dilemma but not the intimacy struggle. The one does not assume the other.

Thus it can happen that a later-in-life option for more intimate relationships (the option for the non-celibate way of life) may force a denial of the validity of the vocational choice of religious life. The two issues are not the same nor can they be presumed to confront the religious at the same point in time. The option for celibacy is a free choice only when the intimacy struggle has been confronted and worked through. This normally occurs a number of years after the choice of vocation.

The rules regulating religious life give a weak nod of assent to this reality in setting up several time-sequence positions within the training years when assessments and decisions are required of the candidate and of those in charge of training programs. This is only a formal acknowledgment that there is a developmental sequence occurring over time for the variety of decisions that have to be made. The psychological environment which surrounds the training is not calculated to promote resolution of the intimacy struggle; it can be presumed to offer opportunity for further assessment of suitability for the vocational choice of religious life. The decision for celibacy is not identical with the selection of religious life as a vocational objective.

The universal call to chastity promulgated by Christ is a call to psychological integrity but not only that. The role and function of grace will certainly affect one's relating to others. The instruction of Christ to love as He loves adds new dimensions. Our deficiencies are an inadequate understanding of the way Christ did love and a reliance on grace to achieve a genuine relation in advance of our progressing through stages of life where such relational possibilities are normally achieved. Religious life ought to provide the opportunity of continuing personal and communal discovery of what it means to love as Christ loved. One feature of that discovery is that religious are being called to integral psychological relationship because the God they are being called to is a Man. The way they are to come to Christ is through their own humanity. Community must provide opportunity to be as deeply and authentically human as one can at a given time.

The subsequent choices made by very many religious who in recent years have opted out of religious life is worthy of note. To a very large extent they go right back into the same work function as they had been engaged in before. If such choices have a message for religious life it is that the quality of the life seems under challenge. The resolution of the intimacy crisis was apparently not achieved for scores of men and women. Now out of religious life, they confront that crisis, reach a more or less satisfactory resolution and then eagerly take up the same work as performed by religious. It would be a bit cavalier to assume that all of those who remain within the ranks of religious life have resolved the intimacy crisis. A "flight into spirituality" is self-protective and perhaps unassailable because of the "super-natural" nature of its motivation. Nonetheless it could be stulti-fying.

One of the tell-tale indicators of the unresolved intimacy crisis in many religious is the popularity in recent years of en-counter groups. The first wave of enthusiasts for these experi-ences included an unusually high number of religious. More clearly than religious life might like to hear, this phenomenon bespeaks a strong need by religious to confront this phase of normal development even though they themselves may be chron-ologically past the age when resolution usually occurs. If survival and the maintenance of numbers are core concerns, then such encounter sessions would be proscribed for religious life. For it is inevitable that the resolution of the intimacy crisis does not have but one alternative as foregone conclusion. People will opt out of religious life as the result of such experiences. But if religious life as now constituted cannot provide opportunity for resolution of the intimacy crisis, it is a moot question whether it is a contribution to the development of the integral person by protecting him/her against normal progression through stages of life.

What may be a worse situation is the quiet demand on religious that they resolve the intimacy crisis with no allowance made for making mistakes and thereby learning and growing by experience. The false belief seems to be that young boys and girls are non-sexual and that adult male and female religious are non-sexual. The equating of sexual crisis with intimacy crisis is yet another mistake. Indeed they are not the same. Adequate tolerance for mistakes in professional work, for violations of justice in dealing with each other and with the laity is accorded religious life. But there is practically no toleration for errors of judgment within the framework of the intimacy crisis. The severest judges in this matter are the religious themselves. Perhaps this would be a good thing if severity of judgment could be shown to be conducive to growth. On the other hand it may be a curious twist which prevents the life style within religious life from contributing to the resolution of the intimacy crisis and then turns to sit in severe judgment of those whose often fumbling efforts indicate they are struggling with this normal developmental task.

The following chapter will attempt to spell out some of the essential features of love and the love relationship which must be incorporated into the effort to cope with the intimacy crisis.

5

Love Relationships

FROM THE HUMAN STANDPOINT the maintenance of a love relationship requires some kind of exchange between the persons involved. It is possible for a person to be motivated by love, to be a loving person, without establishing any significant measure of relationship. Some dedicated men and women live their lives in religion in this way. Except in the context of common brotherhood/sisterhood or in the context of a non-experienced, life-touching reality of the Mystical Body, many religious go through life without exerting very significant influence on the lives of other people. This is not to gainsay their sincerity; it may evoke some regret at their lack of effectiveness in relating to others. These men and women appear as cold motors in the machinery designed to influence the world for Christ. Yet because of their sincerity, their mode of functioning is unassailable at the level of motivation.

There is some uncertainty as to just how long this mode of life can be expected to be sustaining to oneself. At least in theory we can concede the temporary possibility. For such an individual there is no specificity to his/her love—or so he/she believes. He/she simply loves. And all persons enter equally into this sphere of his/her love. In the past the literature of the spiritual life referred to this as "disinterested love." Under the heading of "detachment" the treatises attempted to exalt this approach to life. Parenthetically, they may have succeeded too well and in so doing caused a slow-down in the human developmental necessity to resolve the intimacy crisis. One can wonder how these approaches to living became such respectable modes of trying to live out Christ's message to human beings. There is little in His message to applaud this approach to the Christian life.

To a psychologist, as perhaps to many others, it is interesting to note that plaudits were given in some earlier treatises to those who can love in this manner. But it may be significant that little attention is given to the reactions of those so loved. The human reaction to being the focus of this "detached" love should be attended to. Very frequently it gives birth to anything but a reciprocation. We are to love as God loves us—which is hardly in a detached manner. Hardly anyone in religious life believes that Christ loves in such a disinterested manner—at least not with respect to oneself. To be the focus or recipient of such a "disinterested love" is to become an object, a depersonalized thing to be loved according to some rules and plans and in order to enable the other person to behave in the right manner. To be loved like that is to become a thing used by the other for his/her own sanctification. It is to be the recipient of a love prompted by duty, by a necessity to love in this manner for the sake of holiness and salvation.

It is to be granted that mankind's effort to relate to God need not be mediated by people. There is some emphasis in current theological writing that this is indeed possible. No attempt is made here to exclude any mode of relating to God nor to place such modes in a value hierarchy. However, within any one mode we can be concerned about the quality and the essential nature of the relationship.

The decision to live in community with others brings with it certain to-be-preferred ways of trying to so live. It is a contradiction to opt for community style of life and simultaneously to choose a mode of relating which is considerably removed from personal relationship. The resolution of such a contradiction would require a particular emphasis on the justification of community living as a personal need-serving, self-serving means of sanctification. Unless the intrinsic human value of personal relationships (if not the very essence of Christ's mandate) is seen, then creating community is a self-deception for it then becomes an ego-serving, somewhat selfish means employed in the individual's effort to become a good religious.

Admittedly it is easier to give expression to these ideas

than it is to give dependable guidelines for the development of personal relationships within community. This is so because there is no neat dichotomy between loving another and having one's own needs taken care of. Loving as Christ loves involves the acceptance of the total reality of the other person—a reality to be illumined and discovered through all the diverse findings of human intelligence as applied in all areas of human knowledge and also discovered in the truths of revelation. And on the other hand, the taking care of one's own needs permits at least a temporary emphasis on the "now" experience of relating and risks the temporary reordering of values. There is a situational disruption of the balance between intellectual, emotional and sexual behavior.

For a variety of reasons, it might be expected that those who enter religious life would be vitally involved in the reality of love relationships. Yet often enough what is demonstrated is an exclusionistic point of view having its roots in an attitude the religious brings to, or acquires within, or is pressured to hold concerning his/her way of life. If religious life is viewed as serving the individual's thrust for perfecting self, as a quest for salvation, then religious life is for his/her benefit. It becomes something that the person uses for his/her own purposes. The religious makes friends, works diligently at assigned tasks, is a strong influence on others, surrounds his/her life with activities which will promote movement towards perfection. There is a selectivity evidenced in the values that he/she is willing to incorporate into his/her value system. This selectivity is something other than a hierarchical ordering of values; it functions on an inclusion-exclusion base. It is a self-centered orientation whose antithetical stance towards community living is manifest in positions of deep prejudice toward people and experiences that are not in accord with the self-serving values that energize his/her life.

For the religious with this exclusionistic viewpoint anyone in religious life not living in accord with this adopted value system is meted the attitude of toleration—often with the thought that toleration is at least a minimal sign of personal movement towards perfection. For this religious, other people have the probability of being roadblocks to his/her quest for sanctity. True they are to be served and, if possible, loved as God's children but in themselves they are of no benefit to this religious.

One of the more restrictive effects of this exclusionistic attitude is the lack of awareness that many of the other religious with whom one lives may be thinking quite different thoughts, may be laboring over quite different uncertainties, may be asking questions which never occur to the mind of this encapsulated religious. There is an insularity possible which precludes being sensitive to what is going on in the lives of other people. One sign of such insularity is the honest perplexity of many religious as to the reasons why so many of their members opted for a different way of life. Amazement, shock, regret, disappointment are often manifest at such decisions. It becomes almost impossible to conceive of someone not thinking along the same insular lines as oneself—though there is never a thought to one's being so insular. It may be a genuine indictment of religious life that such consternation at departures does exist. Many of the religious seen in therapy by one of the authors express strong fear about letting others in community know what is going on in their own regard. There is apparently not much sharing at deeper levels of one's life within monastery and convent walls— or so one might surmise when religious are uncertain as to why some leave ranks.

Beyond framing the honest question there is little additional effort to really discern the reasons for the decisions made. This is a self-protective inactivity for there is the implied criticism that religious life has failed to be the meaningful way of life. Interviews with scores of men and women in the throes of their struggle to decide on continuance in religious life reveal quite a difference in the reasons given by these men and women and the reasons alleged by other members of the religious community. The sense of alienation which this disparity begets is detrimental to a decision in favor of remaining in religious life.

Religious life will continue to lose members as long as this hidden alienation continues. What is happening is that some religious have forced themselves to face the intimacy crisis in a more direct way. Working through this developmental task is very difficult if one has to face it in relative isolation. One could argue that a faith-response is clearly needed if the religious is to accept the challenge of non-intimacy. This is hardly debatable. Yet the reality of human experience and human growth is not exclusively a matter of faith-responses. Further, the appeal to a faith-response as the primary way to resolve the intimacy crisis can have the regrettable effect of implying that there is really only one acceptable solution to the dilemma—a faith-response insuring continuance in religious life, a faith-response with strong emphasis on the self-denial aspect of membership in a religious congregation.

The faith-response undergirding the resolution of the intimacy crisis can direct or focus the life-style of the religious in a number of ways. Some religious live out their religious life as basically a devotion to their congregation. They identify themselves with the history, tradition, works, structures, buildings, locales which mark the development of the congregation. They devote their energies to the continuance and improvement of the functions, prestige and influence of the organization. Under this orientation these religious experience considerable disappointment and even chagrin when a member opts for something different. Such a choice is read as a repudiation of the values embraced by this congregation-oriented religious. In non-clerical congregations of men this orientation results in considerable ambivalence when a man leaves the congregation to enter the clerical state. The religious with the strong orientation to the congregation may outwardly show sentiments of joy at the move of the confrere to the clerical state but conversation within the privacy of the community is often pitched at quite another level.

On the opposite side, if the orientation sees commitment in religious life as centered on people rather than on what is institutional, or if the commitment is viewed as a quest for salvation or an attaining of Christian perfection, then the reaction to the departure or to a change to the clerical state is rather different. Here the response of joy can be genuine. The focus here is on commitment in love rather than on the object of commitment. Rather than looking at the means to be used to live out the commitment, this orientation is concerned with the dynamic motive prompting decision. Here a man's desire for more intimate relationship with God (whether through others or through a deeper experience in sacramental life—or both) secures the joyous endorsement of the religious.

The problem here is that there is no right or wrong orientation to life in religion. What is a bit askew is the demand that others view this way of life in the same way that a particular religious does. This type of demand can issue from any and all religious life ideological positions. But what is even worse is that following upon the recognition of clear differences there is no consequent investigation as to what significance these differences have for the attempt of men/women to live together in community. These realities are simply not addressed to any intelligent, systematic way by the congregations themselves. This is a critical reality in the turbulence in religious life today. Short of being able to solve some of its problems, there is no urgency felt by large segments within religious life to look at these realities. The senior author has been involved with a number of self-studies by congregations of men and women. In such studies the fall-off of involvement or the refusal to cooperate at all renders the huge effort to solve some of the problems almost pointless. Whether apathy or complacency or conviction or fear or lack of preparation prompts such non-involvement may be difficult to establish. But it is of little consequence which motive is operative as far as the results are concerned. In the face of such non-involvement there is little hope that current religious will actively rethink their way of life or, in what is perhaps a more pertinent way to express it, actively live a vibrant community type of existence. At the present moment there is a goal-less kind of drift in religious life. True enough there are numerous religious attempting to find some answers but there are few congregations united in any serious way to quest for solutions and life style. The atmosphere is one of "do your thing if you must but don't interfere with my way of doing my thing."

Under this lack of concern for another, the fabric of religious life will become tattered. People will be severely hurt in the ensuing alienation. Any congregation with a high percentage of apathetic members is a dying organization. Unfortunately there is practically no antidote to apathy under current practices within religious life. No apathetic religious would ever be caught reading this book! Serious minded religious can be clobbered into quiescence by "control-by-guilt" techniques. Their every effort to speak seriously is met by the criticism that such efforts are disruptive, are deviating from agreed upon mode of living, are seeking to change the direction of the congregation, or bespeak a faith-drift by the proponent. If such control procedures are not effective in silencing such religious, there is another reality which brings about that same result. The greatest losses in membership have occurred at the younger age levels of religious life. If there are a few "agitators" within the remaining ranks, it is highly unlikely that they will reach any position elected or appointed, where their views will have a forum. The sheer weight of the numerical superiority of older religious provides a power block which will ensure the continuance of most of the traditional policies. Thus if we read a current trend in religious life towards holding the line or as a newly enlivened trend towards greater conservatism we might be misreading the facts if we take the trend as indicative of where contemporary religious life wants to function. We can wonder how contemporary religious life is if its main claim to relevance is that it is continuing to follow traditional practices. If the numbers continue to drop at the younger end of the age spectrum in religious life, more and more power comes to reside in the older religious for whom change and innovative ideas come slowly.

There is then a self-perpetuating aspect of governance within religious life. What may have even greater consequences for the future of religious life is the self-deluding possibility that election by the congregation would be seen by the new superior as a mandate to hold religious life to what it has been for so many years. Pit that possible delusion against the clear evidence that the average age within religious life is jumping higher each year in significant leaps and it becomes painful to envision the future of religious life.

In speaking of love within the context of religious life, there are two aspects that can be considered though love in itself is not so easily dichotomized. We can speak about God, of one's love of God, of the love relationship that exists between God and the individual. We can also look at the human relationships between the religious themselves.

One of the first things to note about God is that the majority of His message about love is the telling of His love for us; the smaller portion deals with how we should respond to that love. Consonant with human development, one becomes a loving person by first coming to accept the fact that he/she is loved. The child doesn't start out by loving his/her parents, the child comes to be able to trust and to love in return. Psychologically, the child who never received love is likely to be unable to love later in life. What God has told us about love is the account of how He loved us first. Over and over this message is repeated in Scripture. Certain sections of Scripture, with no revelation intended, are simply reiterations of His care of us— they are simply designed to strengthen our realization of His love —that despite all sorts of difficulties in our life, He wants us to "hang in there" because He does love us.

Thus God has given us the essential beginning step in our love relationship with Him. For us humans it is still a challenge to develop this relationship. This development is to be accomplished through His work, His sacraments and through His people. Having taken on the Christ-life consciously and reflectively, we are under the obligation through the years of our life to actively reveal Christ. On this we will be judged. Our life is to love and to make ourselves lovable.

His work and His sacraments, avenues of development for our relationship with God, are mediated through things— the intricacies of the language and the use of signs. And when our relationship to God utilized the avenue of relationships with His people, we again confront a mediated reality. For what people are comes to us mediated through speech, through gesture, through the operation of some functions of the human organism. Despite one's cumulative history which might be expected to give one a rather complete sense of personal identity, it usually happens that a person experiences a sense of inadequacy in the attempt to express self when communicating with another human being. This sense of inadequacy is the consequence of having to function within the limits set by being a human—that communication of self and understanding of the other are mediated undertakings.

At one term of mankind's relationship with God, God relates personally in a total, absolute, irrevocable way of the fulness of what He is. If then there is a difference in people's relationship to God, it is on the human level. The individuating characteristics which might earmark one relationship from another, from person to person, imply imperfect, fallible, temporal, limited being. Such restrictions are not applicable to God and thus the differences are ascribed to the human being who seeks a relationship with God. It is the human being who sets the terms of the recognition factor which convinces him that the other relates in a personal individuating way. It could be that the specification is already there but the person cannot see it. Indeed this specification, as far as God is concerned, is already present in magnificent fullness; we humans often do not see it. For the criteria I use in assessing another's love for me are related to my own backlog of experience, to my maturity, to my growth and development, to my understanding. In responding to His Word, in utilizing His sacraments and in learning of Him through His people I am immediately caught up in mediated experiences tied intimately to my personal history.

The faith response which prompts me to hear and accept

His Word as *intended for me* is helped along by contacting God in and through His people and in terms of the sacraments through which I can grow. Because the sacraments remain constant while the people are changing, active, and unique, there is more faith required to see Christ in the former than in the latter. To be convinced that Christ does love individually, we have to use the Word, the sacraments and the people. Without all three we would be unable to come to the awareness of the faithfulness of the personal relationship.

The current emphasis on personalism in religious life can be viewed as a reaction to the omission of the personal relationship dimension of mankind's attempt to establish the love relationship with God. A danger exists that personalism will seek to carry the entire franchise—effectively downplaying the Word and the sacraments. The fullness of the personal relationship requires all three aspects. Religious life in the past tried to accomplish the fullness by concentrating on only two aspects, the Word and the sacraments. Religious life argued to the oneness of God's Word and little emphasized the uniqueness of the way in which it is heard. For even though religious dressed alike, acted together, worked in a common apostolate, their individual response to the Word was precisely an individual response—even if they did not want to emphasize that truth. Any insistence on the elimination of individuating signs and on community living is understandable if emphasis is to be placed on the Word and on the sacraments rather than on personalism.

But to love another person is to invite them into your own personal history. This invitation brings about an involvement experience for if I really love someone my behavior is altered by that love. Often I do not love because I cannot see how I can invite that person to be involved in my history. For example, if the other is someone who should feed my intellect, and if the other lacks that ability, very likely he will not be incorporated into my history. Men on skid row are not a part of the history of the vast majority of religious. There are various segments of humanity "ruled out" when one becomes a religious.

Many segments of humanity never touch the history of religious life. To that extent they are consciously eliminated. By entering the religious life a person narrows the spectrum of humanity with which his own history will be involved. There is nothing blame-worthy in this truth. A mistake is made if we allow ourselves to think or to claim that we are not selective in our relationships with other human beings. In the Incarnation Christ took all of mankind into His personal history. He left this all-embracing love as the model for His people. Indeed all His people can embrace all humanity. But that is something different from saying that this one person or this group could be so inclusive in loving others.

We are currently witnessing the efforts of many religious to broaden the base of incorporating others into their personal history. What they should realize is that in so broadening the base, it is the congregation which may extend its limit but that the individual religious may just be substituting on exclusion-istic segment of humanity for another in his own personal history. It is at the level of theory only that one can argue his/her love includes all humanity. To match the words with actual experi-ence is quite another reality. At the level of theory we would be hard put to advance any good reasons for not loving everyone but the facts are that we do not. Not until the other is incor-porated as part of my personal history can I say that I love that person.

Unfortunately, because religious life does not as yet know how to deal with the entirety of love and love relationships, it often turns to the service function of its social purpose as the channel for the development of love relationships. The service function is somewhat sacralized as being the manifestation of love of another. The troublesome reality is that this can indeed be true and quite likely is true. The one weakness that can be ascribed to this belief is the tendency to invest all relationships in this one avenue of expression. Unless relationships are directly associated with service they are viewed as interfering with the dedication that should characterize religious life. Pursuant to this objective, more and more of the one-to-one relationships are crowded under the protective umbrella of the institutionalization of the works of charity. To further confuse the situation, the religious concurrently hears frequent warnings about allowing apostolic works to become the central focus of life. Thus a tension is created among various thrusts in life—wanting the one-to-one relationship of more personal involvement, legitimatizing the work function as the proper channel for expressing this need and desire, suspecting relationships developed outside or beyond the work function, concern over interdependence of work and prayer. Numerous writers have published works dealing with these thrusts. We do not intend to add to this abundance of theoretical treatises. After stressing the fact that they are indeed theoretical, we contend that their applicability to religious life is obviously circumscribed by the uniqueness of the person.

6

Community: Traditional Goals in New Contexts

WHILE CONTROL OF RELIGIOUS LIFE by the hierarchy has not been one of active intervention (a status desired neither by the hierarchy nor by the religious themselves), the apparent lack of mutual concern over recent developments and trends within religious life is a life-sapping reality that leads to an increased number of problems. Very few solutions to the uneasiness that both sides experience loom on the horizon. Maybe we do not know or do not care to admit what the real problems are in religious life in this day and age. There is even an isolationism which characterizes the various religious congregations themselves. Its roots lie in a survival motif which can and does take some consolation in the "more stressful circumstances" being experienced by congregations other than one's own. One hint as to the pervasiveness of this survival motif is found in the fact that one of the first questions voiced when religious from various congregations meet is that concerning recruitment. We all hope that we can report our numbers as being proportionately better than any other congregation.

One of the great needs in religious life today is for the emergence of effective leaders. The exercise of leadership is exceptionally difficult in matters concerning life-style; it is not as difficult in matters dealing with job function. In the highly structured religious life where traditionally all authority came from the top down to lower levels, all decisions and positions arrived at by some form of democratic action were regarded as essentially advisory to higher authority. In such circumstances leadership emergent from within and at lower levels is easily viewed as revolt—more or less mild—when it is deemed to touch on matters of government, on matters of obedience, on matters of poverty, on matters of personal relationships. So much of the leadership role is by gracious permission or condescension that the word "leader" tends to be a misnomer. We do admit that a leadership role is possible and in fact is often seen in the job function or professional life of the religious. But a strong centralization of authority and government so narrows the permissible areas of leadership as to render it all but impossible to conceptualize circumstances where leadership on the spiritual life and community life dimensions could emerge. History attests to the fact that great leaders or great reformers of the lifestyle characterizing religious life were able to function only because they had already risen to positions which safeguarded their decisions or had decided to revolt in good conscience against the system as they saw it functioning. We have not as yet met the religious who consciously saw his/her role in life to be a prophet; we have not as yet met the religious who prepares himself/herself in any deliberate fashion for the alienation and ostracism which will follow upon the attempt to think and speak critically of the life-style dimensions of religious life. We have met sincere and honest religious who suffer deeply and silently from the withdrawal of "honor in their own country." A later chapter dealing with reconciliation will address this cruelty to which, it is hoped, the words of Christ asking "forgiveness for they know not what they do" might apply.

Religious life does try to find ways to exercise more of a self-directing role in order to engage itself with and in this world. The birth of various groupings of religious—such as the Conference of Major Superiors, Sisters' Councils, Brothers' Councils, Priests' Councils—reflect this. But it seems true that the lives of rank-and-file individuals are little touched by the activities of such groups. These groups render a good service but it would be hard to argue that a high level of leadership is evidenced by these organizations. Since religious life is not and perhaps never will be organized democratically, these organizations remain relatively powerless since they have no legislative possibilities—to say nothing of the inertia arising from the subtleties of intergroup jealousies.

Left with the task of fashioning a meaningful life-style, religious have experimented with different styles in the course of this quest. The very process which opens up new options for religious life results in an inequity for its members. As new options become available, the effect is to make available to younger religious an increased number of possibilities but the effect in not necessarily the same for the older religious. To assume that such is true is to be forgetful of the process of aging. This is truly one situation wherein we are not all equal. This is at least true within the boundaries of the traditional apostolate. The demands for physical stamina and endurance very likely cut off some alternatives for older religious. As one small example, many older religious do not or ought not drive automobiles. The prevalence of cars, attached to various communities in these days, therefore imparts a greater degree of mobility to younger religious while fostering a sense of dependence in the older religious. Yet to be in the minority of those who drive is to open oneself to the demand for chauffeuring service which can become irritating. Thus there are problems all around the community scene.

One of the life-style options is membership in smaller communities—often referred to as satellite communities. Such communities have become a focus of conflict for religious life today. In some ways it is slightly amusing that so much discussion is centered on this development—as though to suggest that these communities are something new. We have always had satellite communities. If one conceives the motherhouse as the core or heart of a province, then every established house is a satellite community. They may vary in size from three or four to thirty or forty. The difference between the past reality and the present mode is found in the route used to establish these smaller communities. In the past the needs of the apostolate, coupled with the decision of higher authority, established the need for and sanctioned these communities of varying size. Today the satellite communities find their origin within the ranks of the religious themselves. Apart from whether it be informed zeal, a desire for deeper spirituality, or experienced dissatisfaction which prompts such decision, the fact that the thrust comes from within the ranks is the difference between past and present.

It is a delusion to invest our hopes for the revival of religious life in such a movement. History tells us that we have had such small communities for centuries. If small communities hold any promise for religious life, it is not because they are small. Yet more and more religious press for such satellite communities. A clear picture as to why is not yet available though some loud pros and cons are being distinctly voiced. We feel that it is important to address these arguments.

One of the most frequently expressed concerns about the emergence of the smaller communities is the fear that the splintering (and that is the word usually used) will be destructive of the core "spirit" of the community. However undefinable this spirit is, it is claimed to be the glue holding individual congregations together and distinguishing them one from the other. There is a fear that smaller communities by reason of their increased numbers will dilute this community spirit. In a strongly centralized government, regulations could help to foster and maintain life-style and behavior, could contribute to a commonness of action giving birth to a commonness of attitude, expectation, cooperation—the mysterious thing called community spirit. When decentralization was adopted as a value, there were immediate and inevitable impacts on the stability of community spirit. Endorsement of the value of decentralization meant the insertion of a new challenge to the maintenance of a congregation-wide similarity of spirit. A congregation can be expected to face up to the consequences of its own decisions even when those decisions are in the nature of an ordering of values it seeks to implement. While related to the person's individualized motives for living the religious life, this community spirit is as much the result of such motivation as it is a contributor to the full living of such a life. The logic of the situation would admit that *one* person cannot have this *community* spirit. He/she can only have his/her own. One can be highly motivated to make a personal contribution to others with whom life is shared and to respond to their efforts to enrich his/her own life. If I have a spirit, *I* have it. Hopefully there will be a coincidence or coalescence between that which animates and motivates me and that which performs similarly for the community.

Many communities try to reify this "community spirit" to such an extent that it becomes a control device. Yet it is such a fragile thing subject often enough to the presence or absence of just one religious within a group. Religious life is as prone as any life-style to the error of concretizing abstractions for purposes of explanation or justification. Once an abstraction enjoys years of being talked about as a reality, it acquires a transcendence which safeguards it against attack and challenge.

The impression easily gained in listening to religious speak about "the spirit of the community" is one of some uncertainty and confusion. At times it is the spirit of the founder—a quite personal thing to that founder. Then it is the Spirit of the founder as interpreted/misinterpreted by the immediate followers of said founder. Then again this spirit of community comes to mean the following of certain traditions, certain ways of acting, certain attitudes toward the world and life. In his rubric, the community spirit is behavioristically produced (perhaps even bottled) rather than being a spirit caught. It has little to do with flexibility in the way or manner of living but rather with the fact that life is to be lived in a prescribed manner.

This spirit is usually centered in the motherhouse whether of a world-wide organization, a national congregation, or a smaller geographical province. The motherhouse is the pattern of the spirit of community—otherwise the label is misleading. It was assumed that other houses automatically had the same spirit provided they patterned their life on the motherhouse. This was and is a comforting fiction but nonetheless unrealistic. It effectively ignored the fact that if spirit is dependent upon the doing of tasks in certain ways, then the circumstances of those tasks are crucial in their influence on the manner of accomplishment. When circumstances change, when the situation becomes different there is a correlative effect on the spirit.

It is doubtful that a spirit has much of a life-giving quality when it is more dependent on certain ways of doing life rather than on certain ways of being alive. It is likened to the difference between one's praying these certain prayers in this particular way and one's being a prayerful person. It is exemplified by the difference between being merciful within the limits of a set apostolate and being merciful where mercy is demanded. The setting of bounded arenas for being merciful partakes less of a spirit than does having the freedom to be merciful.

The "spirit of a community" is being challenged theologically as well as psychologically. The theological has two aspects—one a clarification by way of emphasis, the other in terms of a call to deeper spirituality. In the first instance, the challenge is more than a simple though important call to return to the spirit of the founder. The spirit of the community is being challenged by a theological emphasis that has the understanding of our Christian faith as the focus of full living rather than a focus primarily on religious life as the source of full living. To the extent that religious life constantly seeks to expand its understanding of Christian faith will it partake of the spirit of its various founders.

The emphasis on social justice, on the ecumenical movement, on the brotherhood/sisterhood of mankind, and, perhaps more importantly, on the acceptance by the Church of her responsibility for this world have all challenged the traditional understanding of community spirit. If community spirit is circumscribed by rather inflexible ways of doing life, the challenge is the more critical since none of these points of emphasis can ever be neatly packaged for inclusion under well defined apostolate limits. It is easily seen that a commitment to social justice, ecumenism, brotherhood/sisterhood, and the totality of this world defy approaches that are rigid or set by standards of past centuries. The challenge to religious life today is not the challenge, whatever its advantages, to steadfastly work within predetermined apostolate boundaries. It is the challenge of the freedom to be spiritual.

The experience of moving from house to house of a given congregation will soon convince the visitor that there are detectable differences in the climate of the various houses. There is rarely a communality of spirit among houses. And the more numerous are the houses within a province or congregation the more variants will be seen. It becomes almost impossible for a central motherhouse to control or establish a community spirit. It becomes a problem therefore to achieve a oneness of spirit from community to community. But since oneness of spirit has seemed to be such a desirable thing, the thrust for satellite communities immediately brings into the market place of public scrutiny the fact that there is often disenchantment with community spirit. However praiseworthy the desire to maintain good community spirit, if a split in a community results in the formation of two communities, one with and one without this reified community spirit, it seems inescapable to have to admit that this community spirit never really existed in the first place. Whatever was present was beautifully camouflaged and therefore not very real to start with.

It does remain an open question as to how far the number in a community can be cut and still maintain a sense of community. One mistake might be that religious life has become concerned with the very matter of numbers as a partial answer. It would appear to make more sense to be concerned about personal commitment to "other" as the major contributor to community spirit. There is no guarantee that smaller communities will have this mysterious thing called community spirit. Indeed the history of some such enterprises verifies the sad state of affairs that can exist.

The meaning of the term "sense of community" or "spirit of community" is somewhat elusive. It is probably safe to say that in the past this sense of community had scant reference to numbers in community but rather that community could be recognized by similarity of attire, by the apportionment of the day to the regularity of a schedule universally observed, by the communal exercises expected in any house. Sense of community did not seem to have much to do with knowing the other person as a person. Large numbers of religious never discuss what they believe about religious life, about Jesus, about the Church. In support of this statement, one of the authors finds repeated verification in the numerous workshops for religious which he conducts throughout the year. Part of these workshops deals directly with these unexpressed beliefs about Christ and religious life. The surprising aspect is the joy and enthusiasm of the participants at the chance to enter into such experiences with other religious. Sense of community appears to have less to do with knowing each other than with doing the same things together in the same way and usually at the same daily hour. This permits one to claim to be participating in and to be acquiring this sense of community simply by existing in a communal behavioral context. Indeed to be oneself is to challenge that very sense of community.

The alleged divisiveness of the small community movement is a charge which may explain the functioning of the large community more than it highlights problems in and because of the small community. Within the large community problems get lost in the anonymity of largeness. In times of conflict it is psychologically easy to project an explanation onto the non-personal "they," "them," "it"—the personified thing called "community." Such exonerations are much more difficult within the comprehensive unit of the small community. For in this case the "they" is easily identified; all possible antagonists can be named quickly. Confrontation is inescapable. This is one of the salient differences between large and small communities. If divisiveness means confrontation then the small communities can be rightly so charged. If community spirit in the larger houses means avoidance of conflict through the expedient of escape from confrontation then it has this placating advantage. Yet psychology will hold that the psychic drain caused by the repeated suppression of conflict will exact a regrettable toll on the human spirit.

Some important psychological considerations can inform the thinking about these communities. In an age when involvement has become either sought or shunned the larger communities have the unusual ability to accomodate both thrusts. The larger numbers can allow intragroup non-involvement on selected issues. One can effectively choose both the issues and the persons for one's own attention and involvement and for avoiding the other issues and people. This reality can be an asset or liability to the living of religious life—depending on the ordering of values in one's life. Such selectivity is markedly reduced in the smaller communities since the number of alternatives in issues and in personnel are far fewer under normal conditions. To involve twenty people in ten issues is clearly different from involving five persons in ten issues. Doing one's own thing in a large community would not be as influential on the community spirit as would be true in the smaller group.

The other side of that truth is that in larger communities the numbers limit the influence that one person can exert on establishing values and objectives for community living. To be one voice among twenty-five is different in the pursuit of values from being one voice among four or five. The degree of involvement is necessarily greater in the midst of smaller numbers. For some religious this is the primary motive for opting for a smaller community style of life. This group style also calls for more compromise in arriving at common objectives. The chance to be instrumental in defining group values and objectives has an ascendency in the thinking of younger religious which is often difficult for older religious to understand—so acclimated as they are to accepting a priori values and objectives.

Reduced numbers in community necessarily reduce the available channels of input to the idea-reservoir of a community. And since the age span in such small communities has been rather narrow up to the present, the tendency to encapsulate the homestead within one age bracket has a vision-narrowing effect on the community's view of its role in Church and in the world. Indeed, some criticism is voiced that these communities are a movement away from life in that they do not embrace a broad enough spectrum of age levels—as is the case with normal development within the context of family life. Yet if the experience of these small communities does not sense a need for age bracket representation, it is hard to argue that they are missing something important in life. To put it another way, one does not ordinarily prepare for changes in life patterns (to be the future result of growing older) in psychological ways but rather in pragmatic, economic ways. Then when religious are encouraged not to let economic matters assume primary importance they really don't think much about growing older in any forward looking way.

If only there was opportunity for age differences, the members of smaller communities would likely find even richer significance to life. This would be accomplished by way of stronger personal ties as the result of better communication within a small group. Of course this assumes a great deal of willingness, openness and trust. Since one cannot really trust what he does not know, the smallness of the community can provide increased opportunity for the acquisition of these healthy assets to living. Religious life should be a humanizing form of life. To us this seems to imply a need to meet humanity in many stages of a developmental concept of life by surrounding himself/herself with people in the same developmental stage. This situation quietly allows one to use self as the criterion of where others are. The narrowing of vision that this induces makes the person and the community a less viable and influential force in the world. The often fierce dedication to one form of apostolate can stunt awareness of other aspects of life. Religious who deal rather exclusively with the young all their active lives can have incomplete understanding of other age levels. If religious life is to be spoken of as humanizing, then it must be humanizing over the full spectrum of life—serving the old as creatively as it serves the young. It is doubtful that there are many religious who do not wish to die in the saddle rather than in a rocking chair. The creative possibilities for older religious find no circumscription save that imposed by the limited vision of a community.

The acceptance of a developmental concept as applied to the spiritual order as well as the psychological order would at the same time argue to improved chances for the smaller communities to accomodate to this view of life. Since accomodating to a developmental concept is largely a matter of adjusting to individual needs the large communities would have myriad problems in pursuit of this goal. Developmental growth is often the victim of rule and schedule in religious communities. Crises (if developmental needs can be referred to as such) rarely occur on schedule. It is conceivable that given a critical period in one's life, conformity to the schedule would be ineffectual in promoting growth. At the very least, we can ask how another person can be so positive about beneficial results from such conformity behavior for the person in crisis. Those who claim inerrancy in maintaining that specific beneficial results will occur have apparently solved a persistent dilemma involving both theology and psychology—namely the difficulty in differentiating between habituation of behavior as virtue and habituation of behavior as some form of conditioning. Further they seem to have inside knowledge (if not control over) the way our God elects to interact with specific individuals.

The manner in which contemporary small communities are formed also gives us to special types of problems. The usual pattern of forming these communities is by the free choice of interested people. The new community starts out with people more alike in their interests than different. Such similarity tends to mute any discrepancies that might exist. The compelling reasons for forming such communities are rather widely held and shared by these interested persons. It is one of our convictions that the thinking which precedes the establishing of smaller communities, while very defensible and logical, is nonetheless somewhat circumscribed and limited. When the idea of a smaller community initiates with an individual or a group of individuals it would be difficult to dismiss the possibility that such a desire has some selfish origins. Even if the request is solely based on the desire for experimentation, that very desire indicates that the existing community situation is not considered to be the best or the most complete for this individual or this group. This is an instance where the selfish nature which religious consider to be unworthy of them energizes action to try something likely to be a boon to religious life. If one had to wait for totally unselfish motivation there is little likelihood for either growth or change in any form of life.

The counterpart reaction on the part of many in the larger community is more often than not jealousy—jealousy of another's freedom, of the willingness of another to try existence outside the large community. Jealousy cannot be totally separated from selfishness. To try living in circumstances where meals are not catered, where cleaning and maintenance are not done by others for one's ease and availability to have more time for the service of God may present religious life with valid insights so difficult to gain in present circumstances.

Neither the selfishness nor the jealousy need be detrimental to the individual nor the larger community. They must however be recognized for what they are lest the selfishness be one that leads an individual out of religious life, lest the jealousy be a final source of injury to the future of religious life. A little bit of selfishness may bolster resolve to try something different; a little bit of jealousy if properly recognized can be a call for willingness to explore the need for and consequences of change.

Caught up in the heady exhilaration of change and hopeful of renewal of religious life, some religious seize upon certain new values in religious life, while failing to see the consequences of such endorsement on other values. To be specific, the freedom which allows a group of religious to request authorization to form smaller communities is an outgrowth of the quite human value of self-direction, the human value of freedom of choice in those matters intimately related to one's own life-style. Indeed this is a value to which much of our teaching and preaching is committed. But the active pursuit of this value within the context of religious life has consequences which only selectively enter the thinking of those who seek to implement this value.

A necessary corollary to freedom of choice is the freedom of refusal. And it is here that major trouble brews. The formation of smaller communities, usually composed of young, sincere and pollyannic religious, can and often does result in the formation of communities of rejects in the original community. Let us hasten to add that this is not always the case. But when one has the right to opt for those with whom he/she wants to live, he/she also has the right to opt not to live with certain others. What then happens is that we have something new in religious life—communities with a very large measure of autonomy in determining their personnel. One can ask the question whether the larger social organization can continue its traditional functioning under this new mode of operation. Because the answer is not as yet clear, these comments ought not be interpreted as deploring the movement towards smaller communities. But it does seem important to raise the question—and a few more.

Even with the advantages to be realized by having an age-spread in any community, it may be a bit unfair to ask an older religious to join a small community. More often than not these small communities are being set up in small houses or large apartments. No longer are there spacious grounds and property as in the past. If the younger members of the community are out of the house for most of the day and perhaps evenings as well one can wonder what will occupy the attention and interest of the older religious during the day. Granted than an older person of exceptional calibre could be ingenious in making his older years personally significant, it will have to be achieved not *with* the small community but *because* of it.

These small communities normally operate on a tight monetary budget. They have been marvelously successful in stretching the finances to accomplish good works. While genuine concern and charity prompt them to take care of an older member who brings no income into the community, there are consequences felt by that very person. The depersonalizing effect of being cared for by others (particularly if the caring is discharged primarily as a duty attesting to their being a good religious) can be better tolerated in the climate of larger communities where there are likely to be others in the same situation. But it is markedly different in a small community. Certainly the non-employed member does not have the same freedom of movement as others in the community. In America where matters economic have become so influential in the organization of the life style of religious congregations we are in an era where the dollar potential of community members is important—however regrettable such considerations may be. The situation is not likely to be eased in the immediate future. This is so because the average age in congregations is edging ever higher—and no longer by small increments—with the result that the requirement for economic resources to take care of old age and retirement are more pressing. The source of financial stability is the salary of the active religious. With fewer of these people on the personnel rosters of congregations the reservoir of monetary income is shrinking.

The challenges and the psychic demands on older religious who attempt the life in these small communities are great. Years of habituation to the routines of large group living may make it extremely difficult to adjust to the requirements of small group living. Within the larger groups the segmentation of responsibility and the allocation of areas of responsibility can tolerate the occasional reluctance of some members to "pull their own weight." Others can take up the slack so that there is a fairly smooth functioning. In smaller communities the segmentation and allocation is never so well defined since there is so much overlap of responsibility. Life in these communities requires flexibility and adaptability on a day to day basis. In normal circumstances as one gets older one settles into a routinized lifestyle. These modes may have to be denied if one envisions living in smaller communities. Whether it would be fair to require these readjustments and whether it is reasonable to hope that older religious can make them are open issues. Religious like to think of themselves as very open people but they are normally quite set in their ways. Most of them could not adapt to the swift pace of small group living in our changing society. Thus every congregation will have to maintain at least a few larger communities for some years. But it is not too difficult to foresee some troubling consequences of the effort to maintain larger houses if year after year the newer religious prefer the smaller communities. A real tug-of-war between values, real concerns for people, and a vital interest in serving God's people effectively will maintain community life-style as a sticky problem for many years. There will be an increased taxing of the personal resources experienced by everyone in religious life.

The viability of religious life is very much tied to the resolution of life-style within that way of life. Perhaps it has to be admitted that the religious themselves have not seen the complexity and implications of current movements, yet at the same time a satisfactory solution is not had if a decision from headquarters settles the question. What is needed from central administration is definite leadership in honestly confronting all the realities of these movements. What is needed from central administration is the willingness to find directions for religious life among all its members rather than from any selected few. Authority, insight and vision are not normally synonymous terms. What is needed from central administration is not permission "allowing" something to be but rather an encouragement challenging something to become. And then let the chips fall where they may.

Seizing upon newly expressed values in a somewhat piece-meal fashion introduces problems which religious life has not had to face before. Many congregations have recently allowed and encouraged their members to pursue academic studies more consonant with personal interests. That very freedom, endorsed as a "new" value, leads many religious to study in areas of interest to large segments of American society but which can find only very minimal utilization in the traditional apostolic work of the congregation. Having completed a course of study, such religious find little hope of being able to utilize their expertise. More and more they are looking towards channels outside of the traditional apostolate for using their knowledge in service to others. Seeking employment in institutions other than those of their particular congregation they do receive fine offers which seem to hold promise of being new and effective apostolates. The immediate implications for community living are obvious.

Such a situation can be avoided by a strict control over the educational choices of religious. But the wisdom of such control is questionable for a number of reasons. Such control appears to accept the perdurance of our present educational system. It is doubtful if there is a majority who confidently hold to this expectation. Nor are we claiming to be prophets of a contrary expectation—that it is inevitable that the Catholic school system will vanish. We are reasonably confident that however the system perdures it will be an altered system. It does not seem wise to continue to train in a rigid fashion for a system which sufficed up to the present but which will have to change.

The strict control over the educational development of religious is predicated for its justification on the now unrealistic expectation of automatic employment in the professional part of our apostolate. Religious have very definitely entered into the competitive market where competence has ascendency over the placement decisions and prerogatives of the religious superior. The unionization of the lay teachers in our schools is a threat to the economic base of their operation and to the special treatment status of religious. We should expect increased frequency in hearing statements by the religious growing out of a martyr complex which seems to characterize religious as they compete in the public market place. For years they rejoiced in being able to do apostolic work which others were not doing. They were willing to do such work at considerable sacrifice. Now that others are willing to engage in the same apostolate, with perhaps not the same level of sacrifice, religious are upset with their own reduced prestige. To have one's life of sacrifice in favor of others appreciated by those very others is a good thing; to demand that they behave in appreciative or deferential ways casts doubt on the univocal nature of the sacrifice in the first place. The martyr complex response, though understandably human, seems unworthy of them.

What we are witnessing is a movement away from the belief that the worth of the person is imbedded in membership in a particular religious congregation or in the particular apostolic endeavor of that congregation. This movement has continued to grow and to influence more and more of the decisions in religious life. Membership no longer provides a blanket of security in presenting "community" as that which engages in the apostolic work. People do apostolic work; so when the question is asked "Who is the community?" the answer must be given by identifying persons. It is not answered by speaking of buildings, of schools, of apartments. It is not answered by geography, nor by government, nor by authority. It is not answered in the documents of official approval by the Church. It is a question to be answered as directly as the question. Who is the Church? Loud and clear comes the answer from Vatican II—it is Church as a People—it is the community of religious as participants of the peoplehood. With Gabriel Moran we regret the synonymous use of the words "religious life" and "canonically established organizations." But the use of the terms will probably continue. Religious life is not an entity in its own right. It is what those in canonically established organizations manifest in their life style.

If religious life is part of the Church, then it is to be informed by input from those People of God. Yet religious life has been rather steadfastly insular in its readiness to take direction from the People of God who are rather euphemistically referred to as the laity. In an earlier paragraph we referred to the educational preparation of teachers. It is noted that usually the decisions regulating such training are the responsibility of some superior, some office, or some committee. It is rare that the decision-making agency is composed of any but those who are engaged in rendering an important social service to others; it is quite uncommon that any of those so served would enjoy membership on this august body. Religious life has tended to be self-policing, self-reviewing, self-serving. It often passes judgment on the laity; it frequently takes on the teaching role and somewhat thunderously proclaims the *shoulds* and the *shouldn'ts* of life. It aligns itself with a mentality that sees Church in terms reality. It aligns itself with a mentality that sees Church in terms of organizational structures, in terms of roles, in terms of function. It would be a vastly different ball game if religious were ever to ask the Church—the People—what they would want the religious to be. Religious often pose as authorities in family affairs in easily proffering advice and counsel. But how often do religious permit the tables to be turned such that the laity be given the chance to proffer advice and counsel to religious. What insures the acumen and validity of advice in one direction but not in the other?

Psychologically speaking, the uni-directional nature of this peculiar sharing as a People has a partial explanation in that dynamic functioning which takes an oft-repeated eschatological hope and permits it to become a present reality. Religious are convinced that their choice of a life style in response to God's universal call is calculated to bring about a union with Christ. They begin to express this eschatological hope in quite human terms. For example, for many female religious the term "Bride of Christ" becomes more than an eschatological hope (despite deep uncertainties as to its real meaning) and becomes a verbalized conviction in the here and now, often with a ring on a finger to verify it. Having in some sense then eliminated eschatology, religious life easily sees itself as something "different", something "better," as "more along the way."

Some of this magical thinking surrounds the attitude that religious life takes toward the pronouncing of vows in what is called perpetual profession. Until the religious takes these final vows, he/she has only second class citizenship in the organization. This is a reality both by law and regulation as well as in the more controlling arena of attitude by those already professed. Up until final profession, the whole of a person's life, behavior, and even the future is controllable by the expedient of a threat to grant or not grant admission to final vows within a particular congregation.

Fortunately one of the advantages of a small community is that it can prevent the entrenchment of the idea that religious life has indeed "arrived." The smaller satellite communities call for a revamping of spirituality. Such communities will require changes in formation programs. No longer can such programs prepare for the well-ordered big monastery life only. The activities of the small community are markedly different from large communities. And unless formation prepares one for life as it is met and experienced, it is really not formation at all. For large community living one could be formed (though that is somewhat distasteful) to a prayer-life to be entered into in silence, recollection, and peace. For most small communities, prayer is to be practiced amidst noise, interruption, often alone. The theology which argues that prayer is necessary for life is applicable in both instances. But the type of prayer and the time spent in prayer vary from traditional practices for the smaller community. The very differences can contribute to doubts about one's status as a religious, to guilt feelings about the reduction in time spent in praying . We are in a transitional period where the implementation of the theology on the need for prayer results in accomodation pains (perhaps a variant of growing pains) as we move from large group living to small group living.

To train one to expect lengthy uninterrupted periods of prayer when it is highly improbable to even have that opportunity is unintelligent formation. Apparently many religious are concerned enough about the possible loss of the spiritual dimension in their lives to push for some remedial measures. This concern has given rise to the request for the establishment of

Houses of Prayer as a cure for the inroads on spirituality made by this new small group living and by any activity judged to be detrimental to a well functioning spiritual orientation to life. Religious life began within a particular context at specific points in human history. Its mode of functioning was hammered out as the ideal for that particular context. What seems to be happening is that religious continue to hold to the ideal while trying to impose it on the newer context of twentieth century life. Just as the ideal approach to spiritual life was forged out of the very circumstances of the life as experienced in the context of the times, so also is there a need to adapt, to revamp, to adjust to the context of contemporary life—all the while being informed by honest theology as to mankind's relation to God. Every small community will be a failure if it is judged by standards applicable to large communities.

Another very real outcome of small group living and the freedom which it brings is the statistical fact that many religious while living in these communities do reach the decision to choose a different way of life. Their departures are more noticeably felt than would be the case if they had been in a larger community. But the important consequence is not in the personnel game but in the challenge delivered to the very concept of vocation as permanent. There probably is no religious congregation that has a life-terminating perseverance record better than thirty percent. In the absence of a temporary vocation theory, we should have to admit that either these departing religious never really "had" a vocation (in which case our own judgments concerning admission are now suspect) or that they had one but were subsequently unfaithful to the grace of God (a judgment the like of which we were warned not to make). Very likely we concoct the first explanation as a safeguard against having to accept the second. The mistake is in setting these up as inclusive alternatives. As soon as we limit religious life to the plough-handle concept we have only the two alternatives to deal with. Perhaps religious life needs a migrant worker theory to go along with the farm-land ploughers.

If it proves viable, small group living will require a rethinking of the traditional views of obedience. Clearly there is a move in the direction of a more self-regulated life within the small community. Since a neat package of rules and regulations prove to be ineffectual for life in a small group, religious o-bedience will have to be taught differently than in the past. If there is a much larger measure of self-regulation there is neces-sarily less of traditional religious obedience. Many see this development as potentially destructive of the whole of religious life. This may be true if we are again equating religious life with canonical institutions. But we cannot foresee the day when a social institution will be able to function without authority and therefore, for religious life, without obedience. That things will be different is obvious. It is not so obvious as to how they will be different. But at the present moment religious life is being pressured into a great deal of soul-searching concerning the tenets of formation programs.

To many, there is an implied criticism of traditional reli-gious life in the development of the smaller communities. Beyond the simple numbers game, the style of life is more in contact with the world, more in contact with the People of God. To those so engaged, both the religious and the People, this is a value high up in the scale of values for religious life. To the more traditional and more isolated religious, several significant con-cerns stem from this increased contact. They center on the rele-vance, on the value, of the traditional mode of religious life in the world. They invite concern about the contribution to the Church and to the people that traditional religious life is now making. These same concerns are to be addressed to the life style of the newer small communities also. As with most questions, it is not an all-or-none answer that is sought. The troublesome aspect is that of reaching a judgment in the degree of desirable interaction between the people and those in religious life. If only we could set some criteria we could then evaluate traditional religious life and the life of the smaller community. The task is troublesome because the same faith that willingly bound religious life to a past life style can now be used to move the life style to different modes. This ought not cause too much consternation for it can be safely said that most congregations have already moved their life style a few notches away from the vision of the one who started the congregation. The attempt to consciously move a life style in other directions is the precise challenge that is new to religious life. Rome has always been primarily a reactive controlling agent to religious life; in a leadership vacuum where guidelines are not available, all moves in the direction of a change or innovation are understandably viewed somewhat suspiciously. But when one takes personal uncertainty and turns it about so that it is expressed as a charge against the integrity and sincerity of others, the problem is not a theological one; it is a psychological one. What can be even more entrenched is the conviction that there is just one truth, just one way for religious life, that one person or one group has arrived at that truth and has the certainty of its being the only route for religious life. We will say more about the consequences of this stance in the chapter on reconciliation.

Practically all religious, living in smaller communities, report significant changes in the quality and scope of human relationships within and without the community. These relationships have become the rallying focus for both the advocates and the foes of small communities. The advocates see improved relationships as a much needed expression of Christ's love in today's world; the foes see them as too humanistic, too alien to the single mindedness of one's purpose as a religious and as a threat to one's sense of dedication. In the past, monastery and convent walls served at least two useful purposes. For those inside they enhanced a sense of isolation, a sense of dedication, a sense of difference, a sense of controlled and regulated spirituality. For those outside, they also emphasized dedication, sacrifice, protection, but they also invited (or even demanded) certain behaviors in response to those inside. These behaviors included deference, a tacit admission of the spiritual superiority of those inside, a bit of awe when interacting with them, a concern about one's own language and behavior lest offense be given. In present time, it is inevitable under the newer living arrangements that radical changes take place on both sides of the (now nonexistent) walls. The more contact with the laity the greater the vulnerability of religious to the discovery that religious are not ipso facto better than counterparts in the laity. That religious might be or should be better is not our concern at the moment in looking at small communities.

While holding to the desirability of a sense of loyalty and of not washing one's linen in public, we see religious life as having lived on a one-way street in the past. Human suffering, human problems, the lack of love, the malevolent behavior between persons—all such realities for mankind have been fair game to the advice from those in religious life. But the frailties and failings inside convent and monastery walls are kept carefully secreted from those outside. No argument is expressed here that the laity should be privy to community life realities or that they should meddle in the family affairs of a religious community. What is of concern is the separationism which holds that the laity could not or would not understand religious life from the outside.

Whatever the differentiation, the demarcation between religious life and lay life becomes less clear, less definable, less signposted as the result of the life styles adopted by smaller religious communities. Since behavioral differences become less and less apparent those in religious life and those who view it from outside are forced to examine, accept and respect those faith responses which validate and support the living in both states of life. This does appear to be a very important and necessary approach to understanding religious life in our day. What is happening is usually motivated by a sincere faith response.

One of the significant comments made in response to the move towards smaller communities is the statement that one's personal status is threatened by this development in religious life. This admission is reluctantly voiced except in those circumstances characterized by considerable openness and honesty.

The response deserves consideration. In one of its aspects it deals with ideology. If religious life begins to sanction movements of such self-directed, self-organizing, self-selecting kinds, then the centuries old modus operandi of religious life seems to be changing. To have operated under the belief that controlled living in a (fairly large) community is essential to religious life is set to defenses against accepting a new ideology. To see personal choice and selection become a valued mode within the context of religious life is to set resistance to one's changing his/her personal value system. In the absence of any felt need to change one's values or behavior, one does not change. The existence of new style communities with apparent viability poses problems. One cannot concede the legitimacy and viability of new modes without also being pressed to accept the strong likelihood that religious life as we have known it will undergo change and, in consequence, that the individual will also have to change.

The experience of the threat to have to change is limited to those who do not opt for small communities; the members of small communities have not reported any sense of threat. These two realities take us beyond the question of ideology. The sense of threat has roots in a feeling of personal rejection, a sense of being abandoned by significant others, and most prominently an indictment of one's own status as a religious. The desire for small group living has roots in a reaction against the experience of routine, in a hope of upgrading the quality of relationships found to be superficial in large groups, in a search for added significance in liturgy and prayer, in a search for new avenues for serving the People of God. It is rather rare that a small community acknowledges "rejection by others" as the dynamic behind the thrust for this type of living arrangement. Tensions are inevitable during the time that religious life tries to adjust to new life styles. These particular tensions will ease after a while leaving larger unanswered questions to be faced. Some congregations are pretty much through the travail of these tensions; others are still fairly close to the starting gate.

In a large community composed of adults the need for continuing adaptation to others is less pressing than in a small community. One can find his/her own niche in a large community, settle into it rather comfortably, develop personal idiosyncrasies (often with a reputation built thereon) and continue in the same fashion year after year. Whatever accomodating is required in such a community, it is always imposed on new members in the community—not on the entrenched stalwarts. It is this lack of change that becomes the life style which disenchants the perspective of younger religious. There is little call for personal change in larger communities. Things would be so much better in religious life if rights were not an issue. When charity, deference, respect for service and acknowledgment of expertise supplant the defense of rights, any community, large or small, can be a great place for living.

Another reason why small community living is presently a tension in religious life is that in general the religious are not used to making personal decisions. The decision to move out of a large community to a smaller one is a difficult, highly personal one. In the main, the reasons for such a choice remain in the private world of the one making the choice. Even the verbalizations of reasons are frequently thought not to be the basic reasons. This may be true but then the unspoken reasons become fair game for a variety of uninformed guesses. All sorts of interpretations are whispered. The general category sufficing to label all such reasons is the loss of dedication and motivation. Conceding that one could exercise a new option without being less dedicated or motivated is alien to the years of non-reflective acceptance of there being only one way for living religious life. So entrenched is this idea that it is not surprising that no other explanation than loss of spirit and loss of dedication can spring forth as explanatory.

When this interpretation is voiced tensions are heightened. At this point the "sacrificial lamb" view of religious life is advanced in support of the resistance to allow a small group to move out the larger community. There is an emphasis on the obligation (as essential to religious life) of the sacrifice of personal preference in the cause of contributing to a sense of Christian community by remaining in the larger community. As an idea this is invulnerable to counterattack for surely one wants to contribute to Christian community if one is serious about being religious. However, its vulnerability, in the minds of those moving away from the larger community, is found not at the level of idea but at the level of implementation of that idea by human beings. If one wants to use the sacrificial lamb approach to community living, it must extend across the entire personnel of a particular house. In other words, why must those who want to move out make the sacrifice of yielding their desires to the pleasure of those who want the larger community? Could not the sacrifice be equally expected of those who want the larger community? Who identifies the lambs to be sacrificed? Religious life is facing the end of the sacrificial lamb period— at least as it is selectively applied. It has entered a period of confrontation.

Another interesting aspect of the tension is the level of the arguments pro and con. Almost all of them are pitched at the level of concept, at the level of idea, at the level of history. All of these discussions have value. Only foolhardy people would initiate change without considering input from these sources. At the present moment in history we have mainly only a priori arguments pro and con. We have little experimental or experiential evidence of the worth (or lack thereof) of the new life styles. How would religious life deal with evidence of success for the lives of those so engaged in small community? Would concern over the perdurance of the canonical institution override our concern for the Christian life of those who call themselves religious? Would that first concern allow a grudging plaudit for the resurgence of deeper spiritual life but at the same time silently argue for the exclusion of such communities from the parent congregation because they do not fit into the congregation's history? Persons for congregations or congregations for persons?

All such tough questions can be avoided by the simple expedient of denying the existence of any evidence, in theory or fact, that small community life really works. This is the easy course for the gathering of evidence of fact requires a knowledge of the personal life of individuals. When the focus would have to be on the spiritual life of the person the matter of gathering evidence becomes such a judgmental tak that no one feels particularly qualified to claim skill or accuracy. To balance the picture, a similar difficulty would be faced if the task was to gather evidence that the large communities really work in this day and age. They do have *de facto* existence going for them but that evidence is not the whole ball game; it does not address itself to the various criteria by which religious life ought to be evaluated. Some of the criteria are quite objective on the professional side of religious life. It is the elusiveness of evidence in support of criteria on the spiritual life dimension within any community that gives the de facto existence of the larger community a potency of favorable argument.

There is a delicate interplay between the viability of the small community as a contribution to the spiritual life and the particular apostolate undertaken by that community. Without precision in thought one can come to scramble the criteria so as to judge one aspect by standards rightfully belonging to the other. It is certainly true that many small communities have started and later closed. It could be fallacious to use such statistical evidence to argue that religious life cannot be sustained in small communities. The fault may be in selecting a particular apostolate for which religious may not be prepared or which the realities of American culture and social need will not support. The collapse of the apostolic side of religious life in such circumstances is erroneously used if it is claimed to be evidence that religious life cannot be viable in smaller communities.

Very little of the concern and tension about small communities in religious life ever reaches the level of concern about individuals. Usually the evaluations are made at the level of theory, are made in global terms, are made with the support of impersonal statistics. Most of the questions and concerns about this life style have their reference points in government problems, in concerns over poverty, in uneasiness about the accessibility of closer interpersonal relationships with the laity, in the context of ideological threat to other religious made uneasy by the existence of this life style. Such genuine concerns have been openly and honestly discussed. But few inquiries are heard which deal with one's personal evaluation, personal assessment of the new experience, personal judgments about how the life style accommodates to personal spiritual life in this day. There is no guarantee that such questions could or would be satisfactorily answered at this early stage of a new experience. Whatever the reason, if these and other important criteria are not utilized in an evaluation, no complete assessment of the thrust for different life styles can be expected.

Our discussion of community has devoted a great deal of consideration to the phenomenon of small community living. There are several reasons for this. Admittedly, in terms of sheer numbers, the movement toward smaller communities as consciously desired and deliberately planned is only a small movement within religious life. Our treatment might therefore be seen as disproportionate, as unbalanced. Yet it is our conviction that the importance of the movement is found in its persistent tendency to raise crucial questions and sensitive issues for religious life in these times of change. It seems unimportant to us that religious life implements its *raison d'etre* in large or in small communities. What is highly important is that religious life revitalizes itself. If it has to be needled to do that by a movement which may not be totally understood, then the irritant has rendered a great service. This is why we have devoted so much of our writing to this phenomenon. We hope we have spotlighted the crucial issues raised by the movement. If we have, then the soil is tilled for the next chapters on theology and the kingdom.

7

Theology:
Rhetoric or Renewal

ONCE ONE CONCEDES that an area of knowledge is the end product of mankind's own intellectual activity, he/she must admit the possibility of change and development in the body of knowledge so reached. The human science of theology is rightly included. There are new emphases, new interpretations, new conclusions being stressed in this area of study. Without becoming enmeshed in debate over the accuracy of these developments, we would like to stress the importance of seeing that these developments are part of the contemporary context in which religious life seeks to be a viable way of life. Any particular point of interpretation can be met with a categorical dismissal as being erroneous or a dismissal as at least a departure from past understanding and therefore suspect. But it is more difficult to dismiss people as having an evil intent when they share what is their thought on matters theological. There is no way to organize or control theological investigation so that it would be the exclusive domain of any group. In view of this fact religious life is destined to have to cope with continuing developments in theology because this study deals with mankind's relationship in faith with their God and with the People of God.

Faith in the Lord Jesus is a possibility, a condition, and an action only of an alive people within the context of this concrete world. Outside of this world, or beyond circumstances which define it, faith is impossible. Theology is essentially the process and result of reflection on a life of faith precisely in this world. Each person of faith engages in this reflection— some astutely, penetratingly, some in a cursory, halting, timid, humble fashion. But every person of faith does indeed theologize.

In one sense theology is after-the-fact reflection inasmuch as it is a reflection on the faith lived. It does have a focus in history—both one's personal history and the larger history of the world. In another sense, theology is a thrust into the future inasmuch as it is a challenge to further the life of faith. It is valuable and important to see and to accept the fact that theological reflection is something done by sinful people and by no other than sinful people. Because this is true there are consequences and possibilities and realizations which people of faith are asked to accept. Perhaps there will never be a one-to-one equating of our theological understanding and the actual implementation of that understanding in this world. The implementation of a theological understanding is dependent upon more factors than the achieving of a level of understanding. While subjectively one may defend the sincerity of the person or group that claims a logical and unchallengeable relationship between their understanding and their implementation, such a tie is not easily made objectively.

For instance, it is hard to fault the faith-understanding upon which religious life is predicated but it remains a moot question, to be constantly asked, whether the implementation is in accord with such understanding. The failure to recognize this can lead eventually to frustrated idealism, to communal criticism, to depreciation of self, or to unfulfilled expectations— all because the sinful condition of the theologizers is ignored. It would be hard to explain sin except for the disparity between understanding and implementation. Yet in another sense there is something healthy in the lack of a one-to-one equation between understanding and implementation in theology; it is this very lack that keeps theology as a constant challenge to living. Even if the body of theological knowledge was given, there would always be challenge to life in mankind's attempt to implement the understanding. Now, in circumstances wherein even the understanding is being continually refined, the challenge to life is even more open, more demanding of a faith response. And religious life is a part of this new scene even if it would prefer things to be otherwise. Religious life also experiences this continual challenge to life.

This is so by the consequence of the simple fact that there is no religious life apart from people. Modern psychological theorizing stresses the dynamic, the developmental, the actualizing, the learning, the becoming in its attempt to explain human functioning. It emphasizes, though not exclusively, the phenomenological, the existential, the humanistic experiences of mankind as holding the key to explaining human behavior. It therefore finds no difficulty in riding easily with developments in contemporary theology.

Yet there is the possibility that theology will be used in a partisan fashion merely to confirm one's present position, one's present mode of living, to affirm one's present activity. Such cafeteria theologizing, such pick-and-choose efforts to explain and justify one's own position and behavior tolls the death knell of his/her own spiritual life. For the life of faith is lived in this world among growing, becoming, actualizing creatures— creatures not yet freed in their humanity from the consequences of sin. To limit theology to a mere confirming-of-a-present- position function in our life is really a denial of sonship/daughtership with a God of history.

It is our conviction that though theology can and does have as one of its functions the confirmation of our faith life, it remains an incomplete theology if it offers no greater challenge to the individual than to simply confirm the past or the static present. Theology must have the quality of conversion and renewal. It is a conversion and renewal of living—not merely of ways of doing life—not merely of the rhetoric used to express theological reflection. Theology must present a challenge—a challenge to become continually more alive precisely in this given world. Theology can never be far removed from the market place of men and women in this world if only because the faith is lived here and now in this world and not in some other world of their own creation. Neither Pope, bishop, priest, layperson, or religious can create the world in which he/she would like to do his/her theological reflection. The world in which theology functions is the world as it is given to our experience.

Accordingly it is our conviction that current theological development has implications for religious life. These implications touch the areas of self-understanding, future growth and development. This elaboration loses some of its obviousness in holding that theology should rightly be seen as a challenge for the future—a future so uncertain in a rapidly changing world. At best we can only delineate some areas of theological development along with their apparent implications for religious life. There is no attempt to concretize these implications for it would be a task made impossible outside of given contexts in which religious life is to be lived. We leave both judgments as to their validity and possible concretization to the individual reader.

Since it is the human being who theologizes, a fitting starting point would be to consider a fundamental shift in a theological understanding of anthropology. There is no western Christian alive today who does not have among his/her beliefs about self a tenet which holds that he/she is composed of body and soul, two heterogeneous parts. With the soul being the immortal part and the body enshrouded with mortality, there is little problem in anticipating where such a theological anthropology places (and has always placed) an emphasis and a spiritual value. The soul, quite obviously, is the more important. In fact the soul in this understanding only attains its perfection in gaining an ascendency over its tie with the body and gains its ultimate fulfillment in a final definitive separation. The body is viewed as rather alien and eminently dispensable. The spirituality that issues from such an understanding is familiar. The one task is to save one's immortal soul—though who was to do the saving or how the saving was to be accomplished was never quite clear. This anthropology certainly kept the person's gaze fixed on the spiritual but tended to fix that gaze in a singularly individualistic manner. My task—the saving of my immortal soul—is the preoccupation of my life. This focus makes it easier to pray and work for the salvation of anonymous immortal souls rather than for specific persons whose physical appearance and social condition might have complicated matters.

It further allows a concern for others to be played out exclusively outside the social arena. For who could fault my honest effort and desire to pray and work for the salvation of immortal souls. And finally, especially for religious life, human and personal history, along with the world in which they are enacted, are so closely related to beings in this world (i.e., to body) that they assume an unimportance if not outright malevolence. Treatises alerting persons serious about salvation to the dangers to their resolve to be encountered by contact with this world are familiar to most religious.

But today, in great part due to biblical study, the Christian is faced with another theological view of mankind. In this view a person is seen as an indivisible unity, as an incarnated spirit. Man/woman as a whole is the spiritual person. Indeed the spirit is still of importance but no longer an importance that could be expressed as more so than some other part of the person. It is akin to trying to decide which leg is more important to a person's walking. Now the whole person as existing bodily is important. When immortality is now spoken, it is the immortality of the person. No longer can a person deal with others only at the level of their immortal soul because to understand a person is to understand that person as a being-with-others in this world. Accordingly in such an understanding, history and the world take on a much different relationship to the person than would be the case for the understanding of the person as body and soul—the two-parts theory. One's personal history is the backdrop against which a person becomes himself/herself in this one world.

Clearly this is not necessarily a new understanding of human beings. Perhaps it should be called a regained theological understanding. The implications are multiple but we shall limit our considerations so as to align them closely to our purposes in this book. The value of viewing mankind with this regained perspective has both theological and psychological aspects. The perspective values the Christian person as a whole unified person for whose spirituality all dimensions of his/her being are important. It may not be customary to view the person's sexuality as being important to spirituality but such a highlighting is an inescapable consequence of this new theological anthropology. Human sexuality is no longer treated as merely a negative (or at best tolerated) factor of existence or as something belonging only to the body. It now is regarded in a positive manner as integral to man/woman as incarnated spirit. This means that celibacy is valued not as a "giving up" or a "non use" but as a positive and concrete expression of personhood. One does not deny the body so as to allow the soul to be more spiritual. That harkens back to the duality theory, the "temporarily tied" theory, in this soul's effort to gain control over the base sexual inclination of the body. It has taken a long time to learn that denial of integrated beinghood was never a solution to becoming.

Progress down this route was helped by psychology's strong adherence to the possibility of multi-motivated behavior. There were not numerous homunculi at work within the person, each individually chargeable with responsibility for specific motivation. When unitary motivation became impossible to verify and unpopular as explanatory of human behavior, then the complexity and at the same time the oneness of the human person came to occupy the attention of psychology.

One of the realities pressing upon religious life during recent years is that of a renewed emphasis on the individuality of each member. This has come about as self-discovery by those very individuals and by awareness on the part of the community that it is indeed composed of individuals. This awareness moved quickly to deep concern because of the apparent inability or the studied ignorance of many communities to cope with this event. Many saw and still see being an individual as an attack on religious life, as a threat to authority, as a disruption of "community" life, and, in general, as totally alien to present structures and functioning of religious life. Theological anthropology has definite application to this condition. Perhaps its relevance is nothing more than a restatement (or maybe a re-alignment) of priorities and of relationships. For the emphasis upon the radical spiritual importance of person as a unity establishes the individual person as having a dignity and an eternal importance prior to one's entrance into any particular form of religious life. It is not religious life nor any religious community which confers dignity and significance upon the individual. It is rather the individual in his/her free response to vocation who confers on religious life and eventually upon a particular community its dignity. Mankind was not made for religious life; religious life was made for men and women. There are not in this world certain individuals whose existence is to be deeded over to the survival of religious life or whose vocation is to perpetuate the existence of certain religious communities. We hold that in this world there are individuals, whole persons, whose call to serve the Lord Jesus needs a form of life that will not hinder their wholeness but rather provide a life at the service of being whole. It is religious life that must serve the need of such individuals. We hold that religious life is not a necessary form of society and, at the same time, we cannot foresee the day when some of those called to serve the Lord Jesus will not want to band together for such service.

This emphasis is not intended to overly exalt the individual nor to make the expressing of his/her individuality a superhuman, superconsuming selfishness. It is claimed that the attainment of individuality is necessary to a good religious community. A main purpose of community is to contribute to the growth of its members. Since individuals are always in the process of becoming, that very process cannot be foreign to a community. The incorporation of this process as worked out by the individuals is necessary to community. If the life style of a community seeks to curb or make static such thrusts towards individuality, it arrogates unto itself a finality which will prove its own undoing. It says to itself that the becoming of persons is best done in predetermined ways. It effectively nullifies the personal individual history of those who enter that way of life. It affirms that the Spirit may very well breathe where he wills except that due caution should be exercised concerning religious life.

Respect for the individual and the fostering of his/her person-hood have consequences across the full spectrum of religious life. The vigor and idealism of youth would carry as much weight for the future of religious life as the wisdom of age carries in its humble, practical, lived experience. Instead of an apostolate in terms of which one's personhood could be valued in religious life such valuations would be in terms of becoming more oneself no matter what the work. Of what value an apostolate if the individual does not first know his/her limitations and abilities. Psychology attests to the considerable psychic toll exacted by determined adherence to a job by a person who is not prepared or whose abilities do not measure up to the demand of the job. Surcease from these pressures will be sought and often it is those living close by who have to pay the price.

Equally important are the implications of this theological emphasis for the individual in undertaking to live in community. If the intent is to so live within community so as to save one's soul, that individual operates under a selfishness that impairs his own growth as an individual and contributes little to community. There is an even more comprehensive selfishness possible under the anthropology which sees the person as a unity. If soul is my concern, then my selfishness is limited to matters directly related to soul. However if my oneness is in keen awareness, then all experience can be encompassed by a selfishness in the service of this unity. For this reason, the selfishness possible under the very truth being advocated here is the more comprehensive and inclusive. Instead of abrogating all concerns except those enjoined by the necessity to save the soul, a person now functions with legitimate concern about all aspects of his/her oneness. He/she will seek optimal conditions for the functioning of all aspects of his/her humanity. Pressed to achieve these conditions the person finds that such broad concern is fertile ground for the development of a broad and comprehensive selfishness. While the value priority of soul may have been a distortion of reality insofar as it stressed a duality, it did narrow the field of legitimate selfishness. The current emphasis would have us accept that propitious circumstances promoting the spiritual life are no more necessary than similar type circumstances enhancing (say) one's psychic life. This is one of the messages being announced by the thrust towards smaller communities in religious life.

If there are these extensive areas of legitimate selfishness, the only effective bridle to preoccupation with one's own set of rights and needs is the correlative of rights—namely, responsibility. To understand a person in his/her unity, though liberating, redeeming and integrating, is also to regain for that person the full measure of personal responsibility. In our present theological context, personhood is attained only in terms of others, only when others are allowed to be persons in their own right. The purchase of one's individuality within religious life is not alienating, for the more completely one gains perspective on self the more ready is that person to contribute to others. The fields of psychology and psychiatry underscore the crucial importance of relationships between people. The very process by which a human being is helped within these professions is by way of a being-with-another encounter. Even the limited objective of adjustment to life has its chief focus on the relationships between self and others. The human being in his/her unity always remains a being-with-others.

There are also implications, obvious ones, for authority in religious life. No longer can authority deal with people on the simplistic level of authority as the voice of God. No longer can it appeal solely to the "good of the immortal soul" for substantiating and validating its decisions. Now it must make some effort in its appeal for credibility and discipline to the good of the person as person. The exercise of authority along this dimension will require a thorough exploration into the meaning and significance of the term "person as person" if it is to be enlightened and contributory to the development of that person. The good of the person would include his/her physical, psychological and social well being as well as spiritual growth. Authoritative clout will no longer be found in spiritual browbeating or spiritual threat. If authority is to have a measure of clout, it must speak a concern for the whole person, not just a concern for the results of some action for the immortal soul. It must speak of a concern for the total life of the other simply because that total life is his spiritual life—not something apart from it. There is no doubt that many persons in authority have attempted and succeeded in doing exactly this. But frequently authority, when it discovered leadership to be lacking, found easy clout in reverting to the implied claim of mysterious situational access to the wisdom of God. The thinking religious might begin to question the wisdom of divine wisdom only to be told that divine wisdom is not like human's (true) or that God works in mysterious ways (again, true). Yet neither explanation really deals with the issue of whether the command was indeed conducive to the growth of the total person or was directed only to the superior part—the soul.

The awesomeness of the task of superiorship, under the necessity for considering the totality of the human person in the directives issued, is overwhelming. It is so much easier to be concerned with efficiency, peace-keeping, budget control and similar concerns. If the job of some positions of authority and leadership were thoroughly and honestly written, it would be difficult to find anyone to fill the positions. The guidance of the Father and the workings of the Spirit go beyond the person in authority and are more comprehensive than the very limited, prejudiced and fallible vision of any person in authority. Accordingly, in the acceptance of this truth, the individual religious in accepting and confronting his/her wholeness and its accompanying responsibility might do well to face up to the dubious necessity for the ploy of passing on decisions to higher authority. Hesitancy to make the decisions affecting one's own life and the shunting of these decisions up to the next rung of the authority ladder do not contribute to personal wholeness.

Even the ploy of passing the buck for making decisions to higher levels of authority quite obviously is a tactic that enters into the life history of that authority. Here the inaction of one person intrudes into another's life as a requirement for action by that other. When individuals default in their own responsibility and individuality, they set a climate which would permit authority to become oppressive, autocratic and lacking in leadership. There is simply no leadership where there are not people willing to accept their own personal responsibility. Such responsibility is never discharged in isolation; one's own decisions and the subsequent behavior become part of the other's personal life history so long as the two live together in community.

Finally, current theological anthropology issues a call to all human beings to become concerned with the quality of life for people in this world. Under this call the social arena becomes as much a concern for those in religious life as for any other Christian though that concern might be limited as to active social involvement. A stampede of religious into social action enterprises is not necessarily the appropriate response. An awareness of arenas for possible action is needed.

If such awareness becomes central in the perspective of those in religious life, two benefits will accrue. First there will be some who will want to prepare for entrance into these social arenas of apostolate. Second (and more importantly), this awareness will deliver a message to religious life in the contemporary scene—that under the premise that it is the human being as a whole, as a unity, as a being-in-the-world-with-others that should be the Christian's concern, then religious life is dependent on men and women (the laity) for an understanding of itself, of its functions, and its success or failure. An indispensible source of verification, explanation, and direction for religious life is to be found in the other, in the person-in-his/her-world. For example, should religious make a claim to be living any one dimension of the Christian message quite fully (even with official concurrence by Rome), yet men and women fail to understand how this is so given the reality situation involved, then religious would be well advised to read this doubt and to see that their way of life is not accomplishing one of its objectives—that of witnessing to values in Christ's message. Rhetoric, whatever its source, might well have to give way to reality. It is not only "competent authority" to which religious should listen. There is a message to be heard from equally competent authority (the authority of need and hope) of people within this world for whom the Lord Jesus gave Himself.

To be consonant with their own ideals, religious cannot afford the suspect luxury of divorce from other persons in this world. The meaning of religious life will find amplification in the very interaction with this world. A person does not have to like you, believe in what you are doing, or even be hopeful of helping you to teach you something about being a whole person. The wholeness to be found in religious life cannot be any different than human wholeness to be found elsewhere among people. Dismissing suggestions, criticisms, contributions from those "outside the walls" on the grounds that those proffering such do not understand religious life is self-spiteful. It is foolish behavior, no longer defensible when pitted against the truth that our incarnated spirits place us directly among, with, and face to face with each other, feet firmly on the common ground of a very concrete history in this world.

If there is to be a future for religious life (and we firmly believe there is), it will come about only through understandings achieved in what we shall call "interactive complementarity" on the part of religious life and the world of men and women not living the same life style. If the prayer of Christ "that they may all be one" means something different to religious than it does to others, then "oneness" has lost meaning entirely. If the demands of oneness are read by religious as indicating that they have already achieved that unity and are now engaged in inviting others to join in that achievement, then the historical fact that there were no religious dotting his earth at the time of Christ's prayer may give some pause to surety. Rather we see all of us as engaged in the quest for such oneness and as long as some of us have not achieved it, then none of us has.

In general, people concede to religious life a closer union with God than other life styles enjoy. At the same time they also believe that uncertainties, obscurities and risks are minimized in that way of life. They see those in religious life as so very sure and self-confident in having solved the riddles of life. How this unreal perspective became entrenched may be chargeable to religious life itself and to the phrasings of statements from Rome. It does achieve and maintain a distinction that is more imagined than real.

If biblical studies introduced many of us to a "new" understanding of mankind, even though this came as no surprise to our lived experience, they also fostered a crucial theological development in current Christology—a development premised quite seriously on our faith in the humanity of the Lord Jesus. The "new" understandings of mankind and of Christ fit together hand-in-glove. For that reason they have a decidedly important role in the revitalization of religious life. We choose not to ask the theological chicken-and-egg question concerning the understanding of Christ vis-a-vis the understanding of mankind. We prefer to recognize and to stress their complementarity. Though belief in the humanity of Christ has always been a central article of Christian creeds, a great many Christians did little thinking about the implications of the belief either for the in-this-world exisence of the individual Christian or for the man, Jesus, Himself. The humanity of Christ was relegated to a position of relative unimportance in our spirituality. The very fact of our believing Him to be the Risen Lord tended to blur His humanity by way of stressing the oneness of God. Jesus, in one sense, became overspiritualized to the point where we tended to forget that He still is this finite being, this contingent being who remains for all eternity. We forgot that Jesus' humanity has not stopped nor become something other than humanity. Current Christology, in making us confront the real humanity of Christ, does us a great service by making us confront our own humanity. There are several avenues of these confrontations which we can explore.

The dogmatic statement of the Council of Chalcedon (A.D. 451) is a good starting point. This council affirmed that

Jesus in his humanity is like man in all things apart from sin. Though a seemingly simple statement, it holds within its brevity and in capsule form what proves to be the greatest difficulty for many people, namely, to accept in radical seriousness how ordinary the life of this extraordinary person was. It suggests that to identify with the Lord Jesus there is nothing more basic or more necessary than to simply be a human being. It is saying that a person is saved by becoming fully person, not by becoming something other than person. To readers conversant with contemporary psychology this will have a familiar tone in the phrasing.

To be human was for Jesus to be born into an already ongoing history, into a community of other persons, into already given frameworks of thought. It was to suffer the limitations of those frameworks in expressing Himself. To be human was for Jesus to become part of the world, to become part of the process of human history in which a person must move, grow, and come to richer understandings and ever deeper convictions. It was to learn to love and to be loved; it was to learn to become His own person. It was to experience the vagaries of human consciousness, the ignorance common to men of an era, the mysterious nature of life, the ambiguity of the world, the uncertainties in dealing with others, the limitations and challenges of the moment, the decision made always in the now—whether that now is darkness or blinding light, the need to work through the detail of specific situations in life no matter how clear the insight into self, the constant need to grow and to become in each moment more fully oneself, to live and grow through those moments and experiences wherein one does not know, to accept the mystery not as at the fringes of humanity but at its very heart. To be human is to decide in freedom about one's own life, to choose among very real and viable alternatives. Though Jesus as Son of God had and retained the knowledge, power and all-encompassing vision of that Sonship, the mystery of the Incarnation does not permit the fact and presence of this knowledge to reduce the exercise of Jesus' human freedom to some sort of charade or puppetry. He had to run risks; He had to dare to do life as He understood it. He had to make up His mind in each particular instance as to what the Father wished of Him. In other words, He had to pray. As Son of God He knew fully the mission given Him by His Father, as well as its content and consequences. Yet, as Son of God become man, He knew and experienced the possibilities of misunderstanding, of what it is to fail, of how it feels to be betrayed, the pain of rejection, the aloneness of suffering, the experience of being surprised by the Spirit, and the ultimate obscurity of death. If he did not experience such things, how is He like to us in all things apart from sin?

Jesus, as Son of God, remained at all times in intimate communion and presence with His Father. Yet since He lived so truly a human history, aware in adoration of its infinite distance in relation to the Father, Jesus knew the obvious experience of temptation by being made to know how costly it is to be faithful. He experienced that to be faithful is more often than not to be asked to suffer the cost of fidelity—the powerlessness, the poverty, the loneliness, the misunderstanding. He came to know that the price of fidelity is to have one's personal history distorted by the prejudice, the jealousy, the hardened ignorance of another. If not these experiences, how is He like unto us?

He knew what it is to like to be confident in a mystery that does not and cannot coerce the human spirit in matters which escape the explanations of rational sense. In other words, He knew what it is like to be confident not just in *a* God, not just in *a* Father, not just in *the* Father, but to be so confident that he could say *my* Father, as we say *our* Father. He knew the real pain of physical and psychological suffering, He did not have some rational explanation for the existence of suffering; He had not persuasive demonstration of how the terrible waste of human energy, spirit, and life which suffering involves is contributing to the fulfillment of mankind and to mankind's redemption. He knew the same truth we know—that the human being's basic sickness is sin, nothing more. In realizing this truth He suffered as all mankind suffers. If not these experiences, how is He like unto us?

Many Christians, including numerous religious, find these emphases somewhat distressing. They usually express the difficulty by alluding to the possibility that the emphasis tends to make Jesus "too human." Though we can laud the valid and necessary concern that the divinity of Christ might be eclipsed by an over-emphasis on his humanity, we doubt that this fear is an end result of a stout defense of the faith. We see it as the by-product of a learned uncomfortableness in seriously accepting one's own humanity. Up to the present, much of the formation offered in religious life was designed to bridle, downplay, control, instill suspicion about humanity. The Christian's humanity was enervated by an authority that allowed little individual freedom within its self-promulgated structures, was enervated by an all too easy appeal to the Will of God as perennial solution to personal, corporate or social dilemmas, was enervated by a spirituality that oriented the Christian vision almost exclusively to a future eschatology, was enervated by a limited understanding of the sexuality of a human person, was enervated by a stratification of membership in the Church that championed those strata supposedly furtherest removed from involvement with this world, was enervated by an anthropology that tended not only to bifurcate the human being but championed almost exclusively the more abstract part of that duality—the soul. There is little wonder that people find it difficult to accept with any seriousness the more earthly implications of the humanity of the Lord Jesus. If He is like unto us, then applying one's own understanding of self to the Lord Jesus' humanity would enhance our understanding of His humanity. It is perhaps telling of our own appreciation and valuation of ourselves that we find it so difficult to accept the Lord Jesus as truly being a man with a humanity like our own. It is also telling of our overconfidence in authority (or better, its dysfunction in our lives) that we are so ready to reject anything in the Lord Jesus that has overtones of ambiguity, indefiniteness, doubt, mistake—anything else but the clarity of the Beatific Vision. Yet if He did not experience such, how is He like unto us. Further, of what value the authority which robs a person (even Jesus) of personal freedom.

The present fear which entraps many of us in confronting the humanity of Christ is an ironic twist to St. Paul's Christology expressed in Philipians 2:6 ff. For Paul, the Lord Jesus emptied Himself of His divinity, not so as to deny it, but so as to become radically human, radical to the very experience of death. Yet in our difficulty in accepting Jesus as human we try instead to empty ourselves of our humanity as though the Incarnation demanded the rejection of our humanity rather than its acceptance in hope and expectation.

No matter to what extent we might demur, the central fact of our faith remains—that Jesus is like us in all things apart from sin. None of us knows what it is to be human without sin. All of us do know what it is to be human and what it is to be human in a sinful world to whose sinfulness we all make our personal contribution. It is the sinlessness of Christ's humanity that presents us with the ultimate challenge in our human lives. It is the very real, present, concrete creatureliness of His humanity that presents us with any hope of success in our human endeavor, if only because He offers those who believe in Him the power he exercised in his own humanity—the power of a son of God. Given the history of Christianity, the preaching of the Gospel, and the continual need for mankind to be challenged anew, repetition of this core truth can never be overdone.

Since in the Incarnation the mystery of God is accepted in that same humanity as the very foundation of a personal existence, we can never hold that mystery as some kind of foreign or defective form of human knowledge or that mystery is something contributory to human existence only when it is "solved." Whatever its label (love, chemistry, vibes, etc.), mankind holds to the value and function of mystery. To immerse oneself only in practical realities, only in the tried and true, only in what is known to work, only in the comfortable, only with those people and situations which present neither challenge, nor doubt, nor wonder, is to push mystery to the fringes of our lived experience and to delay the task of accepting and entering into our human condition. This tacit refusal distorts reality and thereby extends and compounds human hurt. And it is never just our own hurt, for others are always a part of our reality, always.

The secret, happily not very well kept, to the life of Christ is that His basic attitude towards life and the basic condition that He accepts as fundamental to His being a man, is a radically complete origination from God and as radical a dedication to Him. Jesus' dependence upon the Father meant neither enslavement nor loss of independence but is rather the only way in which a person, any person, will truly gain independence. It is part of the paradox of the acceptance of mystery at the very center of our personal being that we will be independent only in a dependence upon the Father. There have been ways of viewing the spiritual life which would cast union with God into the same mold with surrender of independence. Perhaps we will only learn by reflection on the humanity of the Lord Jesus that union with God and independence in life grow in direct, not inverse, proportion. The human being who would be willing to detach or separate self from the ambiguity, the risk, the pain, the obscurity, the challenge of being human in order to submit these vagaries of life to some "authority" in the hope of escape from such conditions of life (done in the name of seeking union with God) would be hard pressed to find any such pattern in the life of Jesus. Union with God will never be purchased at the expense of dispensing with our humanity. Its price tag is freedom lived, not freedom deeded over—even if the deed is drawn in perpetuity.

To accept the humanity of Christ as decisive to our faith, to accept that Christ is permanently before the Father as a creature like us and, therefore, intimately bound up with the world and with humans, would be to see that there is no involvement with world or humans that does not have to do with Jesus or with the Father or the movement of the Spirit among men and women. This can be said only because in the Christ-event God has filled humanity with Himself. For religious life a conclusion is inescapable. If the full spectrum of humanity presents us with the encounter and presence of God, then a less quick designation of certain areas of possible apostolic endeavor as "unworthy" of religious life, as "inappropriate," or as "dangerous" would be in order. This is not to say that there are not compelling reasons for selecting specific apostolates. But the elimination of areas of possible apostolate based on such characterizations serves more often than not to embalm a conscience or to still an uneasiness over the settled status of the middle-class functioning of our religious life. These labels relegate to some sort of limbo a service to those people considered social pariah, misfits or undeserving. In the past, the dismissal from Catholic schools of the pregnant teen-ager serves as an example. The proposal here is that choice, involvement and continuation in an apostolate always be subject to human need and not simply be based on adherence to a time-entrenched apostolate. It can and perhaps should be asked from time to time whether the rejection of certain apostolates and the clinging to traditional apostolates have more to do with economic factors than plain human need.

The foremost implication of a belief in the humanity of Christ is that all Christians must endorse the affirmation given in Mt 25:40 "And the King will answer, 'I tell you solemnly, insofar as you did this to one of the least of these brothers of mine, you did it to me.' " Set in the given Gospel context this has to do with the most mundane efforts of service—feeding, giving drink, clothing, visiting the sick and those in prisons. To make the point more emphatic, there is no mention that the recipients of the gift of our human response need be believers in Jesus, lovers of Him, sharers in our faith. There is no other condition than the human need of another. This is not some kind of spiritual theory nor does it have overtones of "finding

Christ in the other," "pretending that Christ is in the other,"—
all of which suggest some kind of spiritual game using plastic
overlays of the image of Christ. The other will not be bypassed
to meet Christ. The meeting of the other is purely and simply
the meeting of Christ. This brings the love of God into the
nitty-gritty of life. Loving God cannot be seeking Him as some
kind of idea for one cannot love ideas. Love of God takes the
concrete form of love for a specific individual. In the acceptance
or rejection of our brother/sister we have accepted or rejected
God since God Himself has become that neighbor. This is the
certain and inescapable consequence of the humanity of the
Lord Jesus.

In the specialization of the apostolate by religious congregations, there can remain some question as to whether or
not the "community" in presenting itself as some sort of corporate
individual is liable to forget that it is never above the Lord's
demand upon the individual. If the community finds that due
to its complexity it has become less sensitive to human need,
there can be serious doubt that there is a religious community
rather than an organization for the preservation of this life style.
Should such circumstances prevail the religiousness of religious
life can be called into question. Whenever a social enterprise
moves towards institutionalization, the demands of personalism
tend to suffer. The institution and the community tend to become surrogates for personal responsibility. The service rendered
by an organization tends to become impersonal for, having
efficiency as a goal, the concern is for getting the job done rather
than for the persons for whom the service is offered. The meeting
of responsibilities is often implied in the ideal which prompted
the founding of social organizations. This ideal becomes a self-
propellant taking the congregation through the years of its own
history in allowing the members to believe they are discharging
responsibilities "because that's what we were founded for." The
meeting of responsibilities can also be implied in the very name
by which organizations are identified. The Church is usually
referred to as Holy Mother the Church. The anonymity asso-

ciated with that title becomes clear in any effort to specify what is the Church.

At this point we feel it important to indicate that we have made a decision to limit the discussion of the implications of Christ's humanity to the larger reality of religious communities rather than to explore the implications for the individual who is the Christian and who happens to be a religious. This is not to downplay the importance to the individual. Quite to the contrary, one's individual response to Christ is more important. While maintaining that a future for religious life is intimately contingent on the growth and development of the individual in his/her response to Christ, we have adopted the larger focus of looking at this style of life called religious life. Hopefully a future collaborative effort will address itself to the spiritual life of the individual in greater detail. We feel free enough to cite implications and consequences of theological emphases for the individual insofar as they elucidate larger implications and consequences for religious life itself. The lack of comprehensiveness for the individual Christian is, we trust, rather obvious and intentional and not to be charged against this present writing.

8

The Kingdom

ANOTHER DEVELOPMENT OF IMPORTANCE in current theology, with implications of crucial value to religious life, is a revitalized understanding of eschatology. Eschatology essentially refers to the belief that history issues in a divine act which terminates history and inaugurates a new age, a new way of being. For many Christians the word "eschatology" is a new one in their theological vocabulary—under the assumption that it gains entrance at all. But since they knew it rather as "the last four things"—death, judgment, heaven and hell—and experienced it only as a concern for their personal future after death, the word itself is not totally new in its meaning. Coupled with a theological anthropology of the past that put heavy emphasis on the dominant eminence of the person's soul, it functioned in the context of a Christian spirituality that fixed the Christian's gaze on a future way of being, rendering a concern for this present world of little importance. In expectation of the world to come our condition was one of waiting, enduring, detachment, of "offering it up" rather than on an energizing thrust to do something about present life. The Christian lived for the next world, not for this one. If this understanding of eschatology made any contribution to our present condition it was in terms of challenging us to a good moral life as the ticket to future joys of heaven or, failing an acceptable morality, as a damning to the eternal fiery torment of hell—with the later being a more fertile field for our imagination than the comparatively dull descriptions of heaven. The fire and brimstone sermons are well known to most religious. Reality-based psychological fear is more potent in the service of morality than the more abstract psychological expectation of joy.

However, current considerations on eschatology, drawn in the main from a return to the Scripture, present the Christian with an eschatology that cannot be pushed or relegated to some distant future or some far off heaven as an experience to be confronted in and after death. As a passing comment, it is strange how the "far out" comment of our youth culture means quite the opposite—attesting to the immediate relevance of the action or thought. In returning to the Scripture we are confronted with the central message of Jesus' preaching: "The time has come and the kingdom of God is close at hand. Repent and believe the Good News" (Mk 1:15). This Kingdom or Reign of God which Jesus preached is not a judgment of vengeance on sinners nor a threat of damnation but rather a saving event for sinners. It is "good news," not bad or threatening news. The Kingdom is not some earthly body politic, not some theocracy. It is not some ecclesial structure complete with leaders and the led. It is not something situated in a place or time. It is simply God's rule. It is not something off in the future but something disturbingly close. And it is on the question of the nature of the Kingdom and its closeness that current eschatology depends for its understanding.

In the past it was a common belief, reinforced by our praying the *Our Father*, that the Kingdom was yet to come. The Kingdom of God was identified with the Kingdom of Heaven, located outside this world (where, no one could say) and in a time called eternity. The expectation in a future coming of the Kingdom was solidly established and firmly entrenched. In the main the Kingdom remained a future hope. Upon closer look, the preaching of Jesus does not simply emphasize a future expectation for the Kingdom. Jesus presents the Kingdom as simultaneously already here and as yet to come, as present and future, as already being realized and yet to be realized. The Kingdom is future inasmuch as it is yet to be fulfilled. But the good news is that the Kingdom is here already since the power of God is already effective in this world and its influence already apparent in the humanity of Christ and in the humanity of those who believe in Him.

Without delving into all aspects of eschatology, it is more

to our purpose in this book to turn to the exploration of what the Reign, already present to us, means for the earthly existence of mankind in the here and now.

The presence to mankind now of the Reign of God recasts a very necessary and important thrust in Christian life. The ultimate concern of the Christian can be nothing else but the Kingdom of God. Since the Kingdom (there being only one) is present to all mankind, acceptance of the fact that no particular Church can call for allegiance in the here and now under the claim that Church is a substitute or surrogate for the Kingdom of God in our present condition seems inescapable. Surrogates make good sense only in the absence of that for which they stand as substitute. Confrontation with the Kingdom of God is not something that will happen at some determinate or indeterminate time in the future, thereby suggesting the advisability of a surrogate in the present. The confrontation is happening in the now. A surrogate is not needed. A Church can only be servant of the Kingdom in the here and now, and religious life no less a servant. The Kingdom is more comprehensive than any one Church and it follows that the witness of a Church cannot be circumscribed by its own institutional concerns nor can its service to mankind be hindered by its own criteria of membership.

The good news of the Kingdom of God breaking into the present is not a good news addressed to some elite or select group of leaders nor to some elected, appointed or ordained representative of a people. It is addressed directly to the individual. If Jesus' preaching of the Kingdom acknowledges anything, it acknowledges the urgency and dignity of personal decision and responsibility. The now presence of the Kingdom of God challenges the individual to decision, to a radical decision between God and the world. Because the Kingdom confronts us now, there is no opportunity for delay under the thought that time is available for decision before the Kingdom comes. Nor is there opportunity for abdication, surrender or substitution of that personal responsibility to anyone, no matter what their

claim to authority. Furthermore, the challenge to decision is
not an imperative on the basis of some impending or future end
but an imperative of the reality of the now. It is not a decision
made "because" God's Kingdom might soon come or "because"
you never know when it's going to come. Because the Kingdom
is confronted in this world, the decision for God is not to deny
the world or to void its value but rather to find its value in
God. To turn from the evil of the world and toward God is
one important movement. But it remains incomplete without a
turning back to the world and our brothers and sisters with
the same love-gift of self to the world as is given in the humanity
of Christ.

This individual decision has important communal consequences. Communal constitutions or descriptions, no matter
how beautifully expressed, no matter how theologically correct
their language, no matter how acceptable to ecclesiastical authority, can never achieve by thought, print or approval what
can only be achieved by the present specific action of the individual. Constitutions or descriptions of what a community am-
bitions for itself cannot be mere expressions of eschatological
hope. To be life-giving and life-sustaining, religious life must
be challenged in the present. There must be challenges to individual growth and human potential, to individual becoming.
The challenge of the Kingdom of God in the now of the individual never fits a communal decision. In the past this might
have been thought possible when all people had to defer entrance
into a Kingdom sometime in the future and when the spirituality
of people could be thought of only in terms of their souls. It
is now quite different when the Kingdom of God is demand-
ingly breaking into the present of every human being. That
intrusion calls for personal decisions now, decisions to be made
in terms of all the potential and possibilities of the now, decisions
which because they are to be made in the now involve everything that the person is, rendering it impossible to make an
exclusively soul decision. Past decisions, though indeed part
of our history and critical to marking ourselves for judgment,

are no substitute for present decisions. The yes of the past is never inclusive of the present, can never stand for the requirement to answer in the present. The current understanding of eschatology makes one thing very clear—renewal (and the decisions which prompt it) cannot be "limited to" the timing of organizational decision or the movement of communal government. It follows that there can be no renewal when there is no freedom for the individual.

Where authority, community spirit, or the good of the community constrain the individual's response to the Kingdom there may well be an event variously described as schism, revolt, division of community, loss of vocation, "rejection of God," etc. But it is also possible that such events or movements can rightly be described as reform, a recall to responsibility, an affirming of the Gospel, a return to the founding spirit of the organization, etc. A community buys and sustains its existence quite cheaply when individual response to the Kingdom is seen more as a threat to it than a possible challenge to life. Authority often forestalls such threat by deciding on the limits of response. Yet authority is never a substitute for discernment of God's Spirit nor is such discernment attained by the process of election, appointment or ordination. It is attained by an individual confronting the thrust of the Kingdom into his/her present now and then responding to it, not simply reacting to it. The Church retains its function. Judgment as to the genuineness and proper use of discernments "belongs to those who preside over the Church, and to whose special competence it belongs, not indeed to extinguish the Spirit, but to test all things. . . ."

With the Kingdom of God impinging on the present, there can be no reality called religious life if lived as though it were some kind of life outside of this very real world. There can be no such thing as religious life which could reduce man to a bundle of spiritual needs divorced from the social, physical and economic embodiment of those needs. There can be no such thing as religious life which champions isolation at the expense of brotherhood/sisterhood. The Kingdom of God is not met in some spiritually established world but is met precisely in this world wherein the Kingdom of God is coming into its own. As full consequence of this truth, the social condition of various segments of mankind and the quality of life of people in this world cannot but be a concern for religious life. The decision for God cannot simply be proposed as some kind of consolation for the future, some kind of excuse for neglecting this present world. The decision for God is rather a reason for changing the world now. No longer can we deal with our brothers and sisters as though this was a time without salvation, a time of mere waiting, or a time in which their holiness has nothing whatever to do with their wholeness. The history we are involved in is not simply a history of souls; it is a history of men and women, a history of men and women coming to its term.

Present eschatology does not offer the human being a simple hope for the fulfillment of his/her soul. Such might have been adequate when our view of the Kingdom was so future oriented and when our view of person held that his/her soul was of singular importance while the body was a hindrance tolerated and disciplined. Contemporary eschatology with its emphasis on the presence of the Kingdom now rather than a future fulfillment directs us toward the definitive fulfillment of our human situation in the present. This will happen only when we begin to accept other men and women and ourselves not merely as souls in need of salvation but as persons in need of salvation. Who would want a Kingdom that has nothing to do with their experience of life? Who would want a Kingdom that asks them to forget themselves, their culture, their yearnings, their thirst for justice, their longing for peace? And if we could so forget, what would the Kingdom be like? Would it be a home for us?

It is not the soul which confronts or eventually will confront the Kingdom of God. It is I as a person who confronts the Kingdom now. I confront it in the demands which come upon me every day of my life in the world. I confront it every day in my brothers and sisters. And in my response, I am responding to the Kingdom. In my decisions for response to my brother/sister I am deciding for the Kingdom. It is a decision for my brother/sister, not for his/her soul. We need only reread Matthew 25 to confirm the reality and realism of this decision. We are already involved in the Kingdom because we are already doing unto the Lord Jesus in doing unto our brothers and sisters.

There is a tension inherent in Christian life. It is the tension of the Kingdom already present and yet to come. There is mystery in this eschatological context. With each successive illumination and penetration of the meaning of the Kingdom the mystery is seen as deeper. It is psychologically healthy to get used to the tension of mystery and to turn it into something fruitful for life. Tension is the stuff out of which one is born into Christ, out of which mankind is prompted to action, in which a person is made whole and because of which he/she can mature. To eviscerate a mystery by attempting a consensual explanation is to rob it of its potency to invite men and women to renewed efforts to guide their lives by it. Mystery is robbed of its value by any attempt to excise the difficult.

While theological development cannot be reduced to the singular contribution of any one field of theological endeavor, it can still be safely said that no single field of critical study has added more to theological development than eschatology. The current situation in theology is the product of progress across the full spectrum of theological thought. It is, moreover, not simply the result of theological development in isolation from non-theological study. Philosophy, critical historical study, sociology, and varieties of scientific experience have also contributed. It should be evident that to attribute the present condition of the People of God, whether for weal or woe, to any one theologian or any group of theologians is the height of a simplistic appreciation of the real world. Whether one rejoices in a renewed Church or finds himself/herself longing for a more comfortable past, everything troublesome or sustaining cannot be laid at the doorstep of Vatican II, its bishops (a few of them), its theologians (most of them) or its other experts. Vatican II did not create something out of nothing. It first listened attentively to movements of the Spirit and of men and women within the Church and to the prompting movements occurring within the People of God. Vatican II was also prepared to acknowledge that more and more people are increasingly knowledgeable of the complexities of mankind in this world and also of the developing content of theological knowledge. Though they may not be experts by any means, they do have an expanded theological awareness today (with as much potential for difficulty as would arise from not having such awareness) that has little similarity with the past. With more people, religious and lay, having some knowledge of theology there will be an increasingly critical listening to and evaluation of those speaking theologically. Authority, no matter what its source, does not manufacture truth simply because it is authority speaking. Authority and knowledge of theology are not necessarily concomitant; integrity is not immunity from mistake; sincerity is no substitute for knowing or for not having grown in knowledge. Theology will be tested in the faith-life of people who now know that they are not alien to theological understanding nor excluded from the movements of God's Spirit.

Within religious life this increased availability of theological knowledge has heightened the awareness of individuality and has instilled a confidence in self even in religious matters. This individuality and this confidence allowed the discovery that religious experience is not something had by a select few, nor some experience far off in some mystical future, nor something possible only if all the conditions are just right. Rather religious experience is the personal experience of the Holy, now. This experience becomes a personal introduction to the ambiguity and obscurity often felt in religious life. The person discovers in the experience of the Holy that the ambiguity and obscurity is not due to some dysfunction in himself/herself nor due to lack of dedication or commitment or fidelity to vows. Ambiguity and obscurity can be signs of the Holy as one personally confronts that Holy in his/her life.

The consequence of this discovery (and then its acceptance) is as freeing as it is challenging. It frees the individual from being bound to thinking that there could be or must be a theology or *the* theology which would be the total and comprehensive explanation of the Holy. Explanation, true; descriptions, true. But only one Person offered anything comprehensive and He did it without offering explanations or a theology. He simply lived it. The challenge is a new responsibility to do more than merely repeat what is read or what is heard from the theologically aware or from the theological expert. The challenge is for the person to internalize what is read and heard in responsibility to one's own religious experience. Religious experience is the challenge to the admission of a Presence and an admission to the continuing need to become. It is the challenge to live life with ambiguity and obscurity as essential and integral parts of human experience. A pretense of certainty may be the Achilles heel that the world has discovered as it looks at much of the life in our religious communities.

Religious communities come into existence because of individuals who have religious experience. Communities are individual people who gather because of something they share as individuals. Believing at least tacitly in the fidelity of others to their own experience, they believe that they too will make their personal contribution to living together. There is never a new superindividual who issues from gathering into community or who emerges because of community. In no manner can community ever override, outdo or be better than the personal responsibility of each individual. There is no avoiding personal responsibility in life or in community no matter who or what might be chosen as a scapegoat. For even to select a goat is an exercise of that responsibility. In life there are just no substitutions for me being me. Nor any good reasons not to be.

9

Reconciliation: Now or Ever

IT IS OUR PERSUASION that we have come to the crucial question for religious life in this day and age. That life must determine if it is going to effect the reconciliation of its life style with the movements of contemporary theology and with the demands and conditions of a world that strongly needs a confrontation with Christ. We remain convinced that the reconciliation of a corporate way of life waits upon the personal address of reconciliation in one's own individual life. Clearly, a rigid time sequence is not advocated since the interactive effects of personal effort and community effort are acknowledged. But we will be led to understand the reconciliation of religious life by first looking at how the ministry of reconciliation involves and affects the individual religious. Reconciliation may be considered as divided into an inner private realm and an outer public realm. Yet the distinction is academic, for in reality, reconciliation is a social *and* a personal reality.

In focusing on the inner private realm we become immediately concerned not only with one's self but also with the other anchor of the reconciliation effort. Is it God or a fellow human being? If I talk about my own individual reconciliation with God I shall perhaps have to admit to a singular intervention by God in a very personal way in my unique life. Such may be my view as I look to God. But it need not be reflective of God's grand intent in sending His Son to accomplish the work of reconciliation. Indeed we are reminded repeatedly in the New Testament that there is something different in the reconciliation of mankind with God from that of one person to another person. The former is exclusively initiated by God through Christ. "All of this has been done by God, who has reconciled us to Himself through Christ and has given us the ministry of reconciliation" 2 Cor 5:18. "It pleased God to make absolute fullness reside in Him, and by means of Him, to reconcile everything in His person, both on earth and in the heavens, making peace through the blood of His cross" Col 1: 19-20.

The objective act of God in Christ is the sole basis of the reconciliation of mankind with God. And it must be recognized that the word "mankind" is too limiting when we speak of Christ's reconciling act. All things, including mankind, have been reconciled. The reconciliation of sinful mankind with a holy God surely involves more than the reconciliation of estranged human beings with each other or the reconciliation of a life style to the needs of the People of God. In the first instance, the reconciliation of mankind to God was initiated and accomplished by God in Christ. Mankind neither participated in nor contributed to this reconciling act of Christ—though mankind does indeed receive the effects of this love. Reconciliation comes to us as a gift. Jesus had to do his work in our behalf alone; only then would a reconciliation be possible. The element of mutuality, thought to be indispensible in the human experience of reconciliation, is not pertinent to mankind's reconciliation with God. Reconciliation was effected by God with corporate and personal consequences for all mankind.

We can see in St. Paul and in the Gospel the implication that there are prerequisites to our participating in the reconciliation achieved by Christ. The guest had to have a wedding garment before he/she could participate in and enjoy the celebration—yet the essential nature of the celebration was not dependent on the guest. There is an element of individual responsibility resulting from Christ's loving act of reconciliation. Through and in Christ we have the means for and the actual achievement of reconciliation. What is left to mankind is an involvement in the methods by which that act embraces us in a personal way. We have been given, according to St. Paul, the "ministry of reconciliation." That mandate reveals the individual responsibility flowing out of God's love for us. We are obligated to behave towards God and towards all human beings in accord with this ministry of reconciliation.

Certainly that ministry of reconciliation—by the very fact that we need it, by the very fact that it was mandated—gives voice to the truth that we live in a world of people demonstrating a lack of reconciliation. But this should not surprise us for Jesus knew that the result of His preaching would not always be present reconciliation. "My Kingdom is not of this world" Jn 18:36. "Do you think I have come to establish peace on the earth? I assure you the contrary is true: I have come for division" Lk 12:51. Particular reconciliations are possible in today's world, we would agree. Yet they are but a promise of the total reconciliation that is impossible as things are now. We will always have wars and rumors of wars; we will always have the need for the peacemakers; we will always witness those who suffer persecution; we will always see the "haves" and the "have nots" engaged in struggle. Yes, we are sinful mankind—with all that is implied by that admission of reality. Reconciliation is then apparently to be first lived in its negative aspect—struggle. It is the struggle to redress grievances, the struggle to secure and insure human rights; the struggle between political and economic philosophies. Detente, a popular word in today's world, is accomodation—not reconciliation; it is wary toleration—not endorsement. And yet even detente is a form of reconciliation or at least a movement in that direction in that it recognizes and accepts the right of another to his/her own choices.

While it is admitted that reconciliation is both a social and a personal reality, it is also acknowledged that there is a tension between the two thrusts. The call for reconciliation, when pitched in a formalist perspective or as a responsibility to a collective cause, often skirts the sense of individual responsibility. Championing noble causes (and hoping others will recognize my profile on my white charger) has the effect of exonerating the advocate but may do little in the practical realm. Perhaps all of us have had the experience of living with a religious who is honestly and intensely dedicated to the eradication of some social injustice but whose very dedication becomes an alienating force within our communities. Whose fault it is, is not of concern—the reality of increased lack of unity is the focus of our concern.

It seems to us that often times a critical truth escapes the ken of many who are energized in a personal way to embark on a serious effort to bring about reconciliation on the social order. The very effort, should it succeed, will transform the whole power structure of the society. In the process of transformation, old values, old tenets, old laws, old customs, old traditions will suffer challenge. In the short view, such a situation can hardly be viewed as conciliatory. This is one of the struggles alluded to in previous comments. Reconciliation as a social movement disorganizes the hierarchy of objectives within a society and thereby introduces considerable tension, thereby fuels partisan concerns and interests, thereby casts fire on the earth. It is to be hoped that before a person opts to be a champion of social reconciliation he/she comes to a rather full understanding of self as a person. It is to be hoped that he/she is prepared for and willing to accept becoming enmeshed in a struggle which looks anything but peaceful conciliation. It takes a strong person to risk the jaws of the divisions that Christ came to spread on earth.

Reconciliation is very much tied to the priorities felt to be decisive for the future of a person or for a group. If the person with whom I desire to be reconciled happens to be attacking something that I feel is basic to my future or something that is basic to the social order as I would like it to be, it will be very difficult to effect reconciliation. If the person's stance addresses a less basic issue, then reconciliation may be a bit easier. For example, a religious who argues that for the sake of poverty those in religious life ought to forego their usual style of vacation excursions may indeed challenge the conciliatory efforts to get along with him/her. But the challenge would not be as confronting as that of another religious who campaigns to remove celibacy as mandated for religious life. The poverty campaigner calls for a quantitative refinement of behavior stemming from a basic principle that is widely endorsed. We can probably live with this campaigner. But the advocate of non-celibate religious life is challenging in a qualitative aspect, is threatening to radically change something most of us consider basic to our life style. Reconciliation in this instance is extremely difficult.

The priorities felt to be decisive for the future of a person or a group energize many of the movements seen in society and in the Church today. Any cavalier dismissal of such movements is as inappropriate as is a blind endorsement. We no doubt have probably met or contended with one or more enthusiasts in one or other movements in the Church. Sometimes it would appear as though their advocates shout that they at long last have discovered genuine Christianity—a Christianity which is going to be quite different from the inauthentic, or the misguided, or the incomplete variety with which mankind has been struggling up to the present. It is crucial to our understanding of the whole process of reconciliation that we acknowledge that it is by no means obvious that God must support programs or movements we approve of or absent Himself from those we happen to disapprove. Both sides of that understanding are essential to our understanding. There is no spiritual ideology which enjoys the unconditional blessing of God for God is not about to be restricted in "breathing where He will" by any human judgment. As far as we know, there is no movement in the Church which God has selected as the sole or even primary channel of reconciling power—neither religious life, the married life, or the priesthood. All of us are engaged in the various ministries of reconciliation—if we accept St. Paul. Human endorsement or human opposition to any movement does not bind God to a similar stance. And we do not challenge the sincerity of those on either side; we can hope they will read the implications for reconciliation in the stance they adopt.

To debate whether any given movement is or is not a channel of reconciliation misses the point almost completely. If an intellectual debate is to decide whether you and I are reconciled, then we are not—for there is a winner and a loser. Or at very least it could be said that each participant in the debate is determined to defeat or make a convert of the other—hardly the basis for reconciliation. It militates against reconciliation to say, in effect, to another: "We will be reconciled only if you believe what I want you to believe."

The reader has probably noted that no attempt to define the word "reconciliation" has yet been made. It is one of those words which to some extent becomes defined in terms of the accretions of repeated use. In a more direct approach, if we equate reconciliation with redemption we could get a handle on the term but primarily in our understanding of God's role and God's act in redemption. In other words, the cosmic and the personally individualized aspects of reconciliation would be a bit clearer but the social aspect remains a bit clouded. It is in looking at the distinctive role of the Church that the social aspect is elucidated. The Church is to confront humanity with the good news that God has accomplished marvelous things for mankind, "But now in Christ Jesus you who were once far off have been brought near through the blood of Christ. It is he who is our peace, and who made the two of us one by breaking down the barrier of hostility that kept us apart. In His own flesh he abolished the law with its commands and precepts, to create in Himself one new man from us who had been two and to make peace reconciling both of us to God in one body through his cross which puts that enmity to death." Ep 2:13-18. And in another passage, "He died for all so that those who live might live no longer for themselves, but for him who for their sakes died and was raised up. Because of this we no longer look on anyone in terms of mere human judgment. If at one time we so regarded Christ, we no longer know Him by this standard. This means that if anyone is in Christ, he is a new creation. The old order has passed away; now all is new!" 2 Cor 5:15-17. The role of Church is not merely to reconcile men as citizens of this world but to summon them into God's new order created in Christ.

St. Paul advises us to forego human judgment or at least to recognize its inadequacy in our effort to understand reconciliation. "Peace is my farewell to you, my peace is my gift to to you. I do not give it to you as the world gives peace" Jn 15:27. If reconciliation is not as the world gives peace, what is it? "I have come. . .to make a man's enemies those of his own household" Mt 11:35. St. Paul states that reconciled humanity is a new creation—"now everything is new." Until such time as we fathom the significance and ramifications of that bold statement, it is doubtful if we shall understand reconciliation—except such acceptance as is accorded through faith. Since reconciliation is a gift from God, accomplished without mankind's assistance or concurrence, the effort to understand it or to define it becomes the formidable task of understanding the mind of God. Acquiring the "mind of Christ" is urged upon mankind by St. Paul. Obviously that will be a lifelong task with the certainty of being only incompletely comprehended by any mortal. But our loving God has given us some clues for recognizing reconciliation and understanding some of its features. Those clues are to be found in the account of the prodigal son.

For purposes of clarity and emphasis, a list of the clues is formulated as follows:

a) The father on his own and by dint of his own activity and choice wanted to share his estate with his sons.

b) The son, free to act, lived under the umbrella of the generosity of the father and eventually decided how he would live.

c) After squandering his inheritance, the son "came to his senses." The account makes no mention of the possible action of the Spirit in effecting this new awareness in the son. Apparently the avenue of reconciliation was a human need and a human assessment of personal condition.

d) The "sin" committed remains unspecified. All that is known is that an alienation or estrangement took place. The son opted out of a close relationship with the father.

e) The father made no move to find the son but his stance

was one of readiness, openness, desire, watchfulness. There
is no mention of forgiveness on the part of the father. The
response was a "Quick! Bring out the finest robe. . . ."
f) The significant line is: ". . .because this son of mine
was dead and has come back to life."

In failing to maintain himself within the perimeter of the
reconciled relationship with the father, the son had lost life—
he was dead. In returning to his father he re-entered the new
life, the new creation established by Christ which defies human
expression in any but inadequate terms. The posture of the
father is also clue-worthy of the meaning of reconciliation—not
coercive, not retaliatory, not punitive (Christ has already suffered
all those pains for us)—but caring, joyful, wanting to celebrate.
It stresses the unchangeable character of God's attitude—always
one of reconciliation. The behavior of the father might give us
pause to consider if we are capable of his kind of reconciliation.
Do we surround our reconciliation efforts with all sorts of conditions to be met, with statements of personal rights, with
demands for psychological recompense for injuries and injustices?
Reconciliation is for all mankind and therefore has the
same meaning in the Church and in the world. There is scant
possibility of misconstruing God's intent in wishing that all
humankind engage in the ministry of reconciliation. "There does
not exist among you Jew or Greek, slave or freeman, male or
female. All are one in Christ Jesus" Gal 3:28. Any narrowness
which excludes segments of humanity rends the unity of our
oneness in Christ. The element of mutuality is not pertinent in
mankind's reconciliation with God. It is pertinent as a person
tries to be reconciled with another person. One can call on his
own experience to spot the challenge to reconciliation that exists
between opposing ideologies, between the contents of the various
faiths. It is no distortion of fact that reconciliation between Jew
and Arab is a painful struggle. It is no distortion to wonder
about the feasibility of a conciliatory rapprochement between
Russia and the United States. Can we effect reconciliation with

those who do not wish to be our brothers or sisters? Neither of us is a prophet; neither of us knows if we can be so reconciled. But we do believe it is our charge from Christ that we engage in reconciling acts through faith. It is true that the systems within which people live form an obstacle to reconciliation. From either vantage point, the anti-abortionists and the pro-abortionists are imbedded into systems which present formidable obstacles to reconciliation. Note how quickly the issues settle to the question of human, personal rights. The United Nations Organization (the term may be an euphemism) has an impressive record of accomplishment only in those areas where competing human rights are not central to the problems between and among nations. A form of paralysis overcomes that august body when national rights are at stake.

Reconciliation is often restricted to alienated human beings at least deciding to get along with each other. Unfortunately in one sense this may be accommodation but it is not necessarily reconciliation. This has been seen repeatedly in religious life where any new thrust in these changing times is treated as a problem of accommodation rather than a permissible by-product of reconciled community. There would undoubtedly be a difference were we to accept that reconciliation was and is a divine act *and* a human responsibility. The Will of God is that His reconciling power be manifest in this world through our ministry. It is an awesome burden but nonetheless an inescapable one. We know that Christ taught that the worship of God was vain while we knowingly remain unreconciled with our brother or sister. Perhaps there is no more forceful expression of the need to understand the meaning of reconciliation than that which emerges out of confronting that awesome truth. Am I living alienated from God when I choose to continue to be unreconciled to another human being? Am I merely poulticizing the illness by placing the blame for the lack of reconciliation on the intransigence of my brother or sister?

Reconciliation will not wait for us to find a way to circumvent the pain, the challenge to our sense of self-righteousness, the demand for genuine love that alone can achieve it. The path to true reconciliation is the daily cross forewarned by Christ because it is the call to accept the truth that He first loved us and now desires that we do in like manner towards others. Reconciliation is the challenge of unconditional love because we have all been made one in Christ. Our union with one another cannot be experienced as a pious emotion to be energized in a Holy Year of Reconciliation that we now add as an afterthought to Christianity; it is the *only* means we have to allow the Father to form in us the trust, the care, the love that Christ exemplified and in which He invites us to share.

There are good things that we do in the name of and in the service of reconciliation. We hold impressive celebrations, we formulate and act upon good intentions, we patch up differences through compassion or private remorse, engage in periodic though miniscule acts of fraternity. We can be glad that we are at least doing these things. But experience suggests the distinct possibility that such activities engender a rather widespread inaction once they are completed. In fact there results a further entrenchment of the status quo since we have demonstrated that we *can* get along together and that our intentions are honorable. The theological dimension of reconciliation would have us understand that there is something more to reconciliation than celebrations, desires, hopes, guilt-allaying interchanges. So often after the joy of celebration we retreat to the entrenchments of the status quo—but now with some glimmer of what someday might come to pass.

Our humanity assures us that reconciliation, like all human endeavors, will not insure perfect new relationships. It is self-destructive to believe that reconciliation is a once-in-a-lifetime phenomenon, earnestly to be sought and forever to be a source of untrammeled joy. There is the ever present danger of absolutizing the human desire for good will towards others, of absolutizing the authentic urge to get along with others. Here again we can be appreciative that such needs and desires do find expression in our behavior towards others. But they are not the essence of reconciliation since Christ is not central to those behaviors nor are the behaviors necessarily informed by the theology of reconciliation. We dare not dispute that God may choose those behaviors as channels for His reconciling power but neither can we argue that He surely does.

For reconciliation to have meaning it must have a life. That life is to be explained by something more than political explanations of relationships, sociological analysis of causes of relationships, economic realities influencing relationships, psychological insights into behavior within relationships, that life must transcend the fact of the you and the me and become "us". For reconciliation to work I must give myself to a new relationship. "The old order has passed away, now all is new" 2 Cor 5:17. I must be willing to be what grows out of this new relationship. If I do not expect or anticipate that I shall be different after reconciliation, then my effort is a sham effort; the basis of my effort is one of distrust. We cannot become reconciled in the manner to which Christ invites us without becoming a bit different. We won't be the same after reconciliation as before.

Precisely here we have come upon the central challenge to religious life today—the willingness to become something different (if need be in Christ's plan for us) as the result of taking Christ seriously. It is the challenge to freely and fully accept the ministry of reconciliation, knowing full well that we shall become somewhat changed by that very acceptance. It is the challenge to release the security hold that we have on past practices and honored traditions so as to allow them to become adapted to the breath of the Spirit as He engages us in the ministry of reconciliation.

The aspect of reconciliation we are considering—that of person to person—has a mutuality about it that clearly requires behavioral attestation. However reconciled I might think myself to be in your regard, I cannot expect you to experience it if I do nothing to attest it. Reconciliation depends for its efficacy on the visibility of behavior. There is a need for a perceived relationship between the gestures designed to express reconciliation and the very value to be pursued in reconciling activity. As with all gestures designed to express an immaterial value, reconciliation can become ritualistic leading to modes of behavior which do not invite or arouse reflection. When, in the act of becoming reconciled, two people are free to be themselves, free to interact in an on-going, non-prescribed way, then there is little danger that the exchange will become ritualistic. Reconciliation, if thought to be achievable only through ritual, is already on thin ice. Planned programs with heavy ritualization will cause it to break through into troubled waters.

Reconciliation, if it is at least initially successful, tears people loose from old securities and sets them in new relations. Here in America we are involved in the redress of injustices towards minority groups. Clearly one cannot undo what was unjust without setting up new relationships, without having to yield old securities. Here in America we witness the effort of women to establish themselves in a more equitable position with men. The religious life and especially the men in that life are being summoned to new relationships—not through the spirituality of a movement called reconciliation but through the social justice movements called equal rights and women's lib. Parenthetically, who is to say that God is not using such movements as yet another channel for Christ's reconciling power.

Lest it be thought that achieved reconciliation always has positive effects, we should be reminded that a sense of guilt can be reinforced by the process of pardon and reconciliation. Perhaps that is not a bad thing but since there are two parties required in the reconciliation, it does remain a problem to ascertain which of the two was the guilty party. The role of pardon in reconciliation activity is not at all clear, save in those circumstances where objective norms permitted the identification of the violator. Does reconciliation mean the calling back from error? It may involve that but it is doubted that such calling is its essence. To fault someone for being in error clearly implies that he/she knew better—else how can I call it a fault. I may argue that he/she was uninformed but if I allow my reconciling effort to take on the earmarks of pardon I may be implanting a deep sense of guilt. The more one voices the claim to be on the side of truth, to that very extent the more difficult it will be to enter into any reconciling activity. If the Holy Year of Reconciliation taught anything perhaps it should have been the advice to mute the claim of certitude (while always willing to acknowledge the faith and values we live by) so as to set an atmosphere in which reconciliation may be possible, may be begun.

That atmosphere must include one's personal willingness to see the effort to be reconciled end in failure. To accord oneself the fame of being a reconciler is to minimize the mutuality of every reconciling effort. If you ever spot a human being whose self-appointed work in life is indicated on the placard "Works of Reconciliation Done Here," be a bit suspicious. This practicioner very likely enters the process of reconciliation with the demand that it work. This no-failure, sure success motive courts the danger that such reconciling efforts be nothing more than a superficial patching over of conflicts (thereby successful) while leaving the deeper basic conflicts untouched. It is the act of the Cross (a failure?) which makes it possible for us prodigals to come home. It is possible to *play at* being reconciled as one of the many games people do play through life. Even the work of reconciliation can become the "important work" that I have to accomplish before I die.

To live our lives for results would be to afflict ourselves with continuous frustration. We don't hear Christ's clear warning that He did not come to establish peace on earth but rather the contrary. If in following Christ we are forewarned to expect the daily cross, forewarned to expect division and strife, then it surely is folly to gear the evaluation of the significance of our years of life to the tally of the number of reconciliations we have effected. Our only sure reward is *in* our reconciling actions and not *from* them. Reconciliation entered into for the purpose of gaining something is a distortion. Entered into because that is what Christ achieved and in which He wants us to share, avoids a concern over results; it avoids a preoccupation even with what we "should be."

A tension or an anxiety runs through life, through our religious life, arising from the difference between what "we should be" and what "we are." "We are," through Christ, reconciled to God; "we should be" reconciled to our brothers and sisters. But the "should be" often comes off as an imperative rather than a statement of what God wants for us and for all mankind. We recognize that, in the main, reconciliation is a future-oriented condition for humankind. Our tension, our drive to make reconciliation work comes not from thinking about that future but from wanting to control it, from wanting that future to manifest all the magnificent results of our present efforts at reconciliation. We get caught in deciding now on some irrevocable course of action that will insure and stabilize a great future for ourselves, for the Church, for humanity. Do we ever stop to think that deciding on an irrevocable course of action is a claim that we are wiser today than we will be tomorrow! How often do we preempt the activity of the Spirit in holding that at long last we have found the one technique, the one approach, the one movement, the one spiritual experience, the one social cause that is favored by God's blessing as the only way to go!

If I approach reconciliation thinking that I am the wiser of the two parties, I have severely and sorely missed the adequate base for just such a reconciliation. For then reconciliation becomes a victory of my wisdom prevailing over someone else's lesser wisdom. Reconciliation is not a victory celebration, it is full living with the mind of Christ. It is not an event, it is a condition of existence; it is not an accomplishment, it is a life style; it is not substantive knowledge, it is a posture, a dream, a vision. Reconciliation is not engaged in comparisons as to the level of wisdom, the depth of insight, the astuteness of expression. In reconciling works, neither person is wiser, more intelligent, more perceptive.

The dialectic of reconciliation has an atypical *modus operandi*. Ordinarily new relationships start with an awareness of each other's virtues. We initially spot the many things we like in the other person—possibly because he/she is putting the best foot forward. Then the discovery of faults and flaws ensues—and if there be passage through this discovery phase, then friendship can result. But reconciliation starts with an awareness that something is askew. We are aware of differences, of faults, of flaws, and are then engaged in trying to discover the virtues that argue for the rightness of reconciliation. We try to discover how much the other person is really like ourselves so as to make it feasible to become reconciled. We carefully explore and examine whether reconciliation will in any way infringe on our rights. We often are not as careful and thorough in trying to come to the knowledge of the manner in which what we are, what we believe, the way we behave might be experienced as an infringement on other persons' rights.

True reconciliation demands that this closed circle of defense of rights be broken. I cannot be truly reconciled to another while hell-bent on safeguarding my own rights. It is saying to the other: "Be towards me the way I think you should be, the way I want you to be, in a manner that will protect my rights. Be as I want you to be, then we can be reconciled." We weren't the way Christ wanted us to be when He accomplished our reconciliation. Nor was the father of the prodigal son at all concerned about rights and duties.

A concern over rights gives easy entrance to a concern over forgiveness in the whole reconciliation effort. Both emphases militate against reconciliation. The issue of forgiveness can be considered from a number of vantage points. If the reconciliation is that of person to God, then since that accomplishment was a free activity on God's part we as humans cannot demand forgiveness nor circumscribe the activity of God by making forgiveness a prerequisite for His activity. No human judgment or reasoned conclusion as to the way God must act is binding on God. For our part, we are likely to need repentance but have no control over forgiveness—and therefore would do well to drop the issue.

If we are concerned about reconciliation between humans, the issue of forgiveness can play a negating role. If I am the offending party, must the other forgive me as a prerequisite to my engaging in reconciling activity? If, unknown to me, the other person has already forgiven me, are we reconciled by that fact—even if I am not repentant? If the other person is the offending party, then the entire reconciliation process, whether initiated by the other or by me, is under my control if forgiveness be crucial. I am in a power position; we are operating on unequal footing. I can offer the unequal gift of forgiving when the other cannot do the same (or so I judge) for me.

If we are concerned about reconciliation between people at the level of ideologies held by them, the issue of forgiveness is again a false issue. For both parties believe the other to be "wrong." But perhaps neither is culpable and therefore in no need of forgiveness. Conflicting ideologies, conflicting theoretical positions would involve forgiveness only if in their implementation human rights have been violated. For example, is forgiveness an issue in the question of fealty and obedience to Rome across the various religions of the world? There is a triteness and a smallness associated with a position of "I forgive you for not believing what I believe." There is an arrogance which would suggest that "I forgive you for not believing and accepting truth." Who is this neo-divine I who metes out such forgiveness?

We are guilty of very shortened vision if we hold forgiveness as a focal point in the reconciliation process. For if we do, we pit virtue against fault while, more often than not, identifying our allegiance on the side of virtue. Forgiveness then becomes something to be accomplished; we are succumbing to a "success" ethic in our approach to reconciliation. We are concerned with outcomes and with success as things to be achieved when almost all of our thinking is to be directed towards attitudes, towards postures, towards love. Surely in genuine love, forgiving the other is not a focus of concern. Forgiveness can be a part of reconciliation but it is not of its essence. It is likely to confound our reconciliation if we choose to make it our central effort. The word "forgiveness" does not appear in the story of the prodigal son nor "in the gift at the altar" admonition. We can wonder how we humans keep putting it in.

St. Augustine's words in *Contra Epistolam Manichaei* have a special relevance here:

> "Let those be angry with you who do not know the sights and tears which the knowledge of the true God, even the most insignificant, exacts. Let them be roused against you who have never been turned from their path as you and I have been. As for me, it is absolutely impossible for me to be angry with you. But so that you may never be vexed with me. . .I must ask you a favor. Let us, you and me, do away with all arrogance. Let neither of us, neither you nor me, pretend to have discovered truth. Let us look for it as something equally unknown to both of us. We can seek it with love and sincerity when neither of us has the boldness or presumption to believe it already in his possession. And if I cannot ask so much of you, grant me at least the favor of listening to you, of discussing with you, as with a being that I for my part do not pretend to know."

With Augustine, we think religious life and the People of God ought to mute the differences which separate them from others. We believe that breaking the circle of safeguarding personal rights and the release of the growth potential of love will move us further along the reconciliation route than any careful identification of wherein we are different, wherein we are separated. Respect for person must be at the root of our conviction that reconciliation does not mean conversion of the other to my truth, does not mean indoctrination, does not mean compromise.

Respect for person means something more than becoming aware of the other's thoughts, feelings, and interests for it is possible to take careful account of these aspects of person and yet have and show contempt for him/her as person. If there be both respect and these particular awarenesses, the ingredients for a personal relationship are present—respect for person (general and theoretical) combined with awareness (particular and individualized). What can be called the "me-ness" of the person's call for acceptance cuts across both dimensions—the "me" as sharing personhood with all humanity and the "me" who is highly individualized and not quite like any other human being. Reconciliation must address the challenge to meet the person on both dimensions of his/her existence.

10

Potpourri of Other Issues

THERE ARE A NUMBER OF ISSUES IN RELIGIOUS LIFE that are relied upon to buttress the continuance of certain life styles within religious life at both the community level and the individual level. We think these issues are worthy of attention but, when considered separately, need hardly require a whole chapter for discussion. In this chapter a melange of such issues are discussed with the intention of rounding out the picture of religious life in its confrontation with today's people and today's world.

The witness value of religious life is seen as one of its assets and as a great need for this world of ours. There are ways in which religious life is witnessing; there are ways in which it thinks it is giving witness; and there are ways in which it is not but should be giving witness.

It is theologically true that religious life is witnessing to the eschatological dimension of Church. In practice, religious life focusses so sharply on the Kingdom of God still to come while remaining rather silent on the Kingdom already here and functioning that this way of life takes on the next-world perspective quite rigidly. It adopts practices serving to support this eschatological focus. One such is the protective isolation of dwelling places. It perhaps should be supposed that a similar isolationism is to be maintained in the Kingdom still to come— or will there be a cultural shock to be experienced by religious in those circumstances.

Because the human being is free, it is his/her prerogative to decide which Gospel truths and values he/she will respond to and give witness. Rooted in the Gospel, these values deserve to be witnessed to. If however, those who are to see that to which one gives witness, are at that time searching for an example of a quite different Gospel value, it then is hard to claim the witness reality of the effort. There is, we believe, a particular witnessing required of an age. This age seems to be calling for the witness to brotherhood/sisterhood. This call keeps pace with God's developing revelation. Again defending the right of religious life to decide the channels of its witnessing to Christ, we can challenge the validity of any self-imposed imperative that it *should* be witnessing to poverty, chastity and obedience. If the age and God's revelation seem to be calling for witness to brotherhood/sisterhood, perhaps that is where religious life should be. Also granting that there is no witness norm which says that religious life should witness *only* to what the age requires, it is still legitimate to wonder about the wisdom of witnessing to Christ in a way which the world doesn't understand. Religious life is trying to show Christ to the world. It follows that clues to the readiness of that world to meet and contact Him have real value and, hopefully, will be properly read by religious life. Witnessing is not solely in intention. It inheres at least equally in the way the consequent behavior is read by the other.

If those witnessed to do not understand the content of our witness, the question of what we are witnessing to remains. The argument for the witness value of religious life is rarely tested for validity from people presumably reading this witness effort. Most statements of the witness value of religious life come from its practitioners or from theoreticians or from Rome. It seems odd that there is so little feedback from those destined to be influenced or impressed by the effort of religious life to contribute to their welfare. If feedback is sought from the Catholic population, it can already be expected to be supportive. We may wonder what the result would be if the feedback was sought outside of the constituency which, in the main, already endorses the existence of some sort of witness function.

In our day there may be a need for religious to distinguish what it is they hope they are witnessing from what they are actually witnessing. It may be that it is the sacrificial aspects of religious witness that are emphasized. Religious life must decide if those aspects are to be the focus of the witnessing. As a specific example, is religious life actually giving witness to the *value* of virginity or to the *sacrifices* of virginity? Or again, is religious life succeeding in witnessing to the *value* of poverty or to a possible status of holiness resulting from self-denial? In a slightly different vein, what does the religious habit witness to? Very likely the sequence of responses by one who sees a person so attired proceeds as follows: "This is a religious and therefore I expect such and such behavior, such and such attitudes, etc., etc." It is the inclusion of the "therefore" which should give pause. It indicates that this is witness based on history, based on preformed expectation. The encounter is a step removed from a genuine person-to-person exchange. Membership in the organization may be so highly prized that a religious can adopt historical witnessing without going through the process of decision which makes witnessing to values clearly his/her own choice.

What all Christians are involved in is giving witness to Christ, to the fact that it is possible to live a human life believing in Him and that such a faith-life is open to all people, to the content of His message that present life is not the end of everything, and to the reality that we are brothers and sisters. Granting their sincerity and the value of their choice, religious have nevertheless given a disproportionate emphasis to poverty, chastity and obedience. These counsels are not the heart of the Gospel message. They are a few from among many avenues for expressing the need and desire to witness to Christ. It cannot be gainsaid that history attests to the success that religious life has achieved at times in giving effective witness along these dimensions. There indeed was a basis for the claim that religious life was approaching Gospel living in at least some of its dimensions. Its reputation now becoming established, religious life found it difficult to avoid the "salvation by rhetoric" pitfall that most social organizations meet in their history. The favorable early reputation resulted from the behavior of the people actually involved. Rhetoric touches a life style at the level of concept;

it is a step removed from the existential reality of what is actually transpiring. It seems to us that a congregation that has to dig into its past history or has to rely on dusty treatises at headquarters to validate its present witnessing is courting this salvation by rhetoric approach to life. The verbalizations of what a congregation is doing are never quite as convincing as behavioral validations.

A hypothetical illustration may underscore these possibilities. There is no religious congregation that would ever want to be guilty of not responding to grave human need. If hungry unfortunates present themselves in asking for some food, the congregation wants to respond in giving food to the hungry. Yet for reasons of efficiency and economy, many large religious communities turn over the operation of the kitchen to catering firms whose policies do not include such unanticipated dispensing of food. Depending on one's values and point of view there is or is not a problem here.

If the testimonials to the witness value of religious life comes largely from believers, perhaps questions should be raised about the value. Usually favorable argumentation comes from within the Church or within religious life. This is an encouragement in the faith and therefore such argumentation has a positive function. It is the overextension of the declarations that is difficult to spot. That religious life becomes preoccupied with a concern that it be witnessing may not be a healthy sign. Intellectual preoccupation about witness gives rise to a question about the reality of execution.

Obviously religious life does not have the entire franchise in the market of witnessing to Christ. Every true Christian is engaged in that happy reality. Very frequently religious life puts forth an argument intended to differentiate its witnessing from that of a lay person "in the world." It is conceded that the person in the world (where else?) may be giving witness to Christ but it is maintained that religious life is still doing it uniquely for it is more clearly incorporating the eschatological dimension in its witnessing. It is very likely theologically true that religious life affirms the eschatological dimension. But eschatology, with all its offshoots, is theological rhetoric both valuable and important. But a person does not witness to theological statements, a person does not witness to rhetoric.

It is our conviction that the whole question of witness is intimately related to the matter of vows in religious life. For the moment we are not concerned with the nature of the specific vows taken in religious life but rather with the activity of vowing within that life as that activity has relation to witnessing. Witnessing to Christ is so directly tied to the realities of this world in its present history that one of its salient characteristics is flexibility and adaptability. Witnessing to Christ has its behavioral outlet in realities and situations of this world. While there is a certain across-the-board list of human needs in every historical period, it has to be admitted that specific times call for specific witness responses. Thus whatever tends to fixate the type of witness from age to age, across the changing history of the world, also tends to limit and severely reduce the very witnessing so desired. Thus in one sense it can be regretted that religous life ever decided on vows as necessary to its life style. The vows may hinder the honest religious from moving towards the fullness of what they feel they must be, their fullness in Christ. Espousing social causes, participating in legitimate marches and demonstrations because there is where Christ is to be witnessed to, are often denied to religious by reason of the vows or the interpretation thereof. This is an irony of Christianity that the very means taken to witness more fully to Christ come to be limiting to the ability of the person to do just that. It is one of the tensions in religious life, not to be solved by simple edict from above.

Witnessing to Christ involves behavior motivated by certain beliefs. The vows of religion do not add anything to the deposit of beliefs. If there be a person caught up in the scope of the Christ-event in his personal history, there is no demonstrable necessity for vow in his/her life. There is a dynamic quality about his/her response to Christ that would certainly prompt behavior to be consonant with the objectives of the vows if not to their specification of means. The vows for that person would make behavior a duty—thus downplaying the dynamic motivation characterizing his/her response to Christ.

If one day the religious of the entire world were to be notified of an edict from Rome abolishing all vows, what would happen to religious life? Should we expect a pell-mell rush to change the style of that life? If so, what would be said about its present witness to Christ? If such be the expectation, then the vows are essentially a matter of government. In fact, vows are a historical reality and historical oddity in the Church. There was little or no concern about vows until the eleventh, twelfth and thirteenth centuries; there was not even a theology of vows until people started to make vows.

The deep concern of religious life about preserving the crucial importance of vows lest its very existence be put in jeopardy, puzzles the psychologist more than the theologian. Why do religious need the hierarchical ordering which puts the vowed person a notch above the sacrament person (i.e., the married person)? Very possibly there is an important reward value to vows. Because the vows subjectively accomplish this ordering they may have additional importance. The ethic that voluntary sacrifice should have its reward—even prior to parousia —may be operating here. The focus is on the sacrifices and not on values.

Vows can also serve as crisis-bridging supports. When crises in life fail to be ameliorated by extensive human effort, summoning the reinforcement and support of spiritual values and eschatological hope could be an effective move. Yet very few religious would like to concede this support role as a primary function of vow. In another sense vows seem to indicate that religious life needs firm evidence that a person is serious about wanting to witness to Christ. Perhaps the person is not to be believed on his/her own but if that person will only vow to God then he/she will be believed and accepted. This apparently underlies the practice of refusal to allow anyone not in vows to be a member of a particular congregation.

With witnessing firmly tied to one's own personal history, the argument in favor of considerable flexibility in religious life for manifesting different types of witness appears sensible. That life also thrusts for uniformity, for singleness of mission, for regularity of community activity, for conformity behavior across the gamut of ages and talents. The thrust seems to be towards having this community give corporate witness. But it remains a moot question if viability can be maintained under the thrust for corporate witness better than it can under the emphasis of individual response to Christ. For a Christian, at least as a hope, there are no restricted channels for his response to Christ. For the Christian in religious life, there are restrictions on possible channels for manifesting his/her love of Christ. It must always be the concern of those in religious life to make an on-going assessment of the restrictiveness of the channels. Religious life must allow a person to be creative with his/her life and its disposal before the Gospel. The disposal of individuals before the Gospel will give to the group to which they are associated a powerful and persuasive charism—the charism of the power of love.

11

Conclusions

IN A BRIEF SUMMARY, we would like to state the basis for our optimism about the future of religious life. Much of what we have said reveals the roots of our optimism. Whether from the theological perspective or the psychological perspective, the current emphasis on individual worth, on the value of person over institution, on the call to a personal responsibility for there to be corporate witness, on the necessity to mute differences in engaging in the ministry of reconciliation—all are viewed as revivifying life. As these emphases gain foothold in religious life that life style can become a renewed channel for witnessing to Christ. Because we have insisted on the crucial importance of the now in life, of His Presence now, we cannot blind ourselves with a fret about the future. Very likely that future will require religious life to be different. But unless we are trying to pre-empt the Spirit we would do well to address the future as firmly rooted in the reality of our now experiences. The guiding image chosen by Vatican II for a renewed understanding of Christianity was the People of God. The vision and constructive possibilities for an understanding of the present and the building of a future are to be found in those People. The People are called to life by Christ. Each individual shares in the charismatic structure of the People. If religious life adopts this view of Christianity, its future is assured. There are signs that the process is underway.

No spiritual renewal of any Church or any gathering will occur until the individual is spiritually renewed. It is our conviction that growing numbers of individuals in the laity and in religious life are accepting that responsibility and will not be put off from that goal. They are willing to accept only what is commensurate with the depth of responsibility they personally experience. Both wholeness and perfection depend on the quality of life to be had in any situation. The invitation to wholeness and to love is all the more fetching when people are invited to contribute to their realization. When the individual is allowed the participation, allowed the experience of that dimension of responsible living, then the viability of the social organization seems assured. Further, the individual who accepts responsible participation is serious about his/her own spiritual renewal.

We see religious life becoming aware of the need to incorporate all its own members in its own pilgrimage, becoming aware that it is a co-equal partner with all the People of God and cannot separate itself from them. Under the impetus of developments in theology and in psychology we see the individual in religious life taking a greater command over his/her own life along with acquiring a greater understanding of how that life is inextricably intermeshed with those in his/her community and all people in the world. For these reasons, as well as others, we willingly say "aye" for a future for religious life.

An Interesting Thought

The publication you have just finished reading is part of the apostolic efforts of the Society of St. Paul of the American Province. A small, unique group of priests and brothers, the members of the Society of St. Paul propose to bring the message of Christ to men through the communications media while living the religious life.

If you know a young man who might be interested in learning more about our life and mission, ask him to contact the Vocation Office in care of the Society of St. Paul, Alba House Community, Canfield, Ohio 44406 (phone 216/533-5503). Full information will be sent without cost or obligation. You may be instrumental in helping a young man to find his vocation in life.
An interesting thought.